One Summer Dream

by Daniel K. Steelman

SILVERSMITH
PRESS

Published by Silversmith Press–Houston, Texas
www.silversmithpress.com

ISBN 978-1-967386-58-1 (Softcover Book)
ISBN 978-1-967386-81-9 (eBook)

CONTENTS

ACKNOWLEDGEMENTS

Thank you, Terry, my wife. I haven't publicly spoken the words I love you to my wife since our wedding vows thirty-nine years ago, but now seems the time to do just that. Loving, forgiving, supporting in all I have ever done, her wisdom has shone through in all our struggles. It's hard to imagine someone who came into my life so unexpectedly and has shared so much. That's why I will say I love you, Terry, and I always will. For this I can be grateful. Thanks for all your help.

Pastor Jesse Stokes—his energy comes from one source, the Savior of the World, Jesus Christ. Without Jesse's encouragement and energized enthusiasm about this story, it would have never happened. As I have stated and have now come to the conclusion, the Lord puts people in your life and His timing will always be perfect. Thanks, Jesse, for making this Summer Dream come to life again, Amen.

My good friend Kelly has always been a private individual, not worrying about the noise around him. It's actually hard to be that kind of a person in today's world, which is why I admire him so much. He is true to himself and exists on his own terms, which is a blessing to those around him. Thank you, Kelly, for including me in one of your adventures. That adventure became part of who I am.

Kelly O'Neill, Terry Steelman, Pastor Jesse Stokes

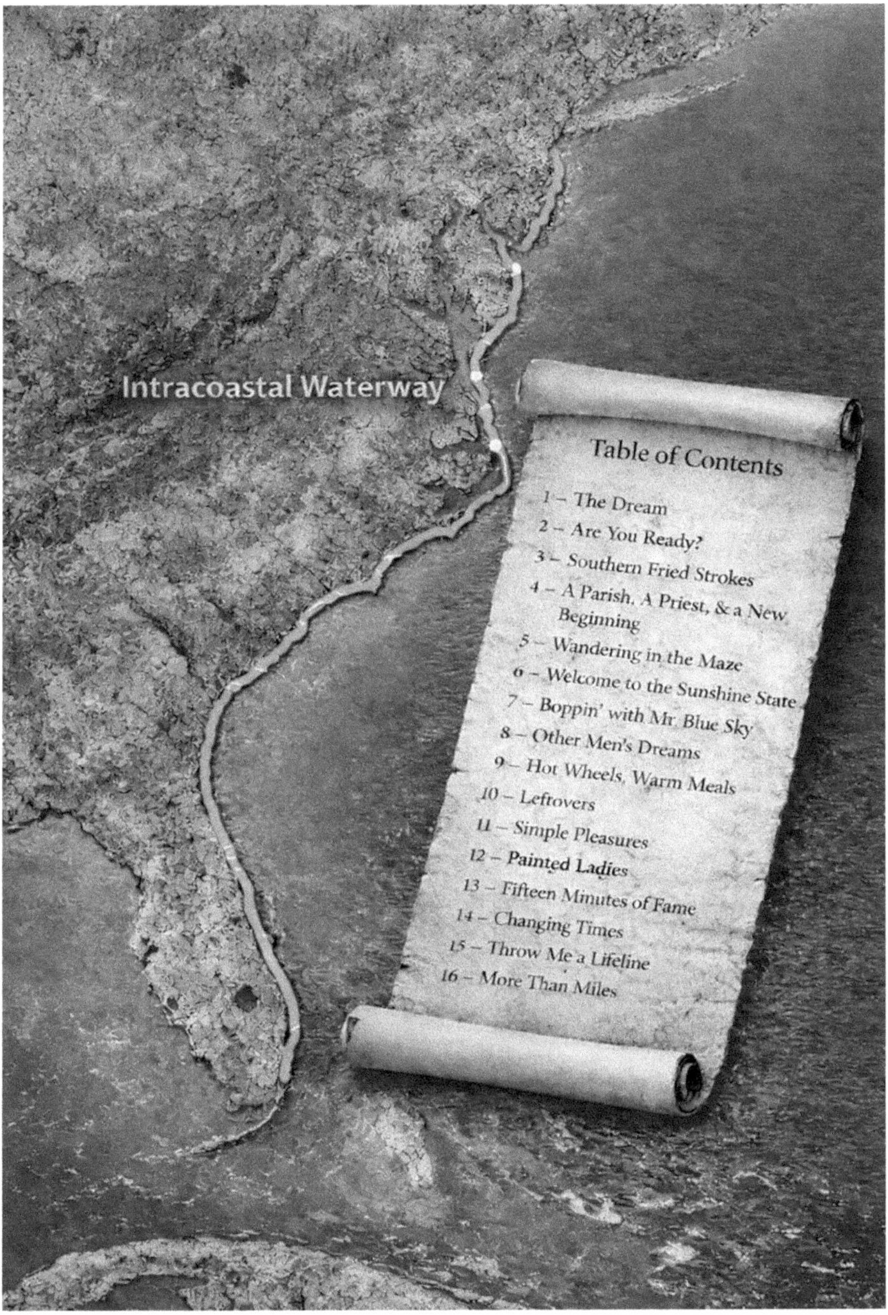
Intracoastal Waterway
Table of Contents
1 – The Dream
2 – Are You Ready?
3 – Southern Fried Strokes
4 – A Parish, A Priest, & a New Beginning
5 – Wandering in the Maze
6 – Welcome to the Sunshine State
7 – Boppin' with Mr. Blue Sky
8 – Other Men's Dreams
9 – Hot Wheels, Warm Meals
10 – Leftovers
11 – Simple Pleasures
12 – Painted Ladies
13 – Fifteen Minutes of Fame
14 – Changing Times
15 – Throw Me a Lifeline
16 – More Than Miles

Chapter 1 - The Dream

It was the summer of 1978. A different world. A different time. When I look back on it now, it feels almost like another planet—slower, looser, less watched. Summer was everything. You spent all year waiting for it, imagining what it would bring. I guess that part hasn't changed, but back then, when summer finally arrived, it was like the whole world opened up.

I grew up in and around the beach. My father was a lifeguard in Ventnor, NJ, and from the time I was two years old, I was on the sand. The ocean, the water, the beach—that wasn't just where we went; it was part of who I was. It felt ingrained in me, woven into everything.

When I was little, my dad would put me to sleep in the lifeguard tent. I can still remember lying there, eyes closed, half drifting off, listening to the sounds outside—the steady hush of the surf, people's voices, the random shouts, the seagulls, that whole jumble of beach noise that blends into its own kind of music. That sound put me to sleep as a kid, and I never forgot it.

Summer became the season where all of that came

back. The smells, the sounds, that sense of anticipation—What's this summer going to be? As we got older, summer took on a new flavor. Now we could drive. We could gather without checking in every second with our parents. We had our own world on the beach—our friends, our routines, our stories. It really did feel like its own little society.

By that point we lived in Longport, NJ, on the bay. Water was everything. My dad wasn't a fisherman and he didn't care for motorboats, but he loved wooden boats and he loved to row. That was part of his legacy to us. My brother took to it, but I think I loved it even more. Rowing just made sense to me—simple, honest, physical, close to the water.

Looking back, it feels like all of that—those summers, that water, those sounds in the lifeguard tent—was quietly getting me ready for something I had no idea was coming.

Near the end of that summer of '78, on a rainy evening, a bunch of us were at our house in Longport. It was one of those nights when the weather shuts everything down, and you end up inside with your buddies, talking, laughing, telling stories. It was me, my brother, a couple of friends, and my next-door neighbor, Kelly O'Neill.

Now, Kelly wasn't just any neighbor. Our houses were practically glued together, separated by an alleyway maybe three or four feet wide. He had a brother and two sisters; I had my brother. Someone was always out on somebody's porch. Their place sat right on the bay, with a big porch that seemed to attract people like a magnet. If it wasn't Kelly and his friends, it was his sisters or his older brother Tommy and their friends. The O'Neill's house was one of those homes where something was always going on.

That night we were sitting around, having a couple beers, just messing around, not thinking about anything serious. Then Kelly made an announcement. "You know what, guys?" he said. "Here's what I'm thinking. At the end of the summer, I'm gonna take a lifeguard boat and row down to Florida." We all reacted exactly how you'd expect a bunch of young guys to react to something like that—laughter, wisecracks, all kinds of nonsense. "Yeah, sure you are." "Right. You and who else?" "What are you gonna do, stop halfway and hitchhike with a boat?" The usual. But Kelly didn't back down. "I'm dead serious," he said. "Totally serious. I'm going to do it. And you know what? Who wants to go with me?" There was more laughter and more teasing, but underneath it, the question hung there.

I'm pretty sure my brother got roped into saying he'd go, at least at first. But at that time, he was just out of college, and I don't think he was ever really serious about it. I think he was humoring Kelly. Truth was, none of us thought it would actually happen. It felt like what it was—a late-summer pipe dream, the kind of thing you say when you don't want the season to end. Summer is winding down, you don't want to let it go, so you start dreaming up ways to extend it, stretch it, turn it into something bigger than itself. That's what this sounded like. The night ended. Everybody went home, still laughing about "Kelly's big idea." But the thing is—it stuck with me.

Over the next couple of days, nothing more was said about rowing to Florida. Life went on. I went to the beach. But that idea wouldn't leave me alone. I kept thinking, "Why not?" We were out in boats every day. I had spent hours upon hours in rowboats as a kid—no engine, just oars—pulling myself through the back bays of Longport, fishing all day, then rowing home. It didn't feel impossible to me. Hard, sure. Crazy, maybe. But not impossible.

I finally went to my brother. "You're not really going to do this, are you?" I asked him.

He admitted it. "No. I'm not. And Kelly's not going to either. There's no way."

I said, "Why? Is it really that crazy?"

"Yeah," he said. "It is that crazy."

A few more days went by. I kept thinking about it. Turning it over. Testing it in my mind. Finally, I went to Kelly. "I'm your guy," I told him. "I'm going with you." He didn't hesitate. He was 100 percent in, all over again. Suddenly the thing that had been a joke in a roomful of guys became real between the two of us.

We celebrated quietly in our own way—because, really, it wasn't that big a production for us. We lived right next door. We were always wandering back and forth across that little alley, drifting onto each other's porches. Our lives were intertwined that way. The word started to leak out that we were serious. People still didn't believe us. To most, it was still that same silly dream, two kids trying to hold on to summer. I talked to my father about it. He surprised me.

"Yeah," he said. "Go for it. Do this."

He wasn't a fisherman and he didn't like motorboats, but taking a lifeguard boat and rowing an astronomical number of miles on some wild adventure—that lit him up. He loved the idea. That was his blessing. But there were limits. "I'm 100 percent behind you," he said. "But you guys have to figure it out."

That meant everything: how to pay for it, how to get a boat, how to get gear, how to actually make it happen. We didn't make much money in the summers. We had a little, but not enough to outfit a long trip. And we didn't even have a boat to row. That was the first big obstacle.

Without a boat, nothing else mattered. It kept the whole dream feeling just out of reach, elusive, like something you could almost touch but not quite.

Back then, adults weren't hovering the way they do now. People would let young people fail, try again, figure things out on their own. No one stood over us with a neat plan and a checklist. The attitude was more: "If you want it, go find a way." So that's what we tried to do. Nights, we'd sit and talk. I'd have a pad of paper and a pen, trying to get Kelly to throw his ideas out. "What are you thinking?" I'd ask. "What am I thinking? What are you thinking?"

At the time, there were only a few casinos in Atlantic City. The casino business there was very young. The streets and surrounding communities were now alive with possibility—older residents wondering how they might wisely invest, younger people eager to build a future through new jobs, and gamblers arriving with dreams of winning big. That atmosphere of hope and momentum became part of our brainchild, giving us the chance to believe we could ride with that wave. We started to ask ourselves a new question: What if this could be a promotion? We figured maybe—just maybe—someone would pay attention to two kids in a lifeguard boat. So we came up with a rough idea: we'd promote Atlantic City and the casinos by rowing to Florida. We had nothing more than that. No business plan. No written proposal. Just two kids with an idea and a lot of nerve.

"Okay," we said. "So that's it. That's the angle. We go to the casinos and pitch them. We tell them we're going to row from Atlantic City to Florida and promote the town. Two guys in a boat. That's the show."

We honestly thought that might be the fireworks

everybody would gravitate to. Now when I think about that, it makes me chuckle. But back then, it was all we had. Kelly had the car. I had a motorcycle. If we had to go pitch someone in person, we had wheels of some sort. So we started with the only real tool we had: a phone and the Yellow Pages. Resorts, Caesars, Bally's. We circled numbers and started calling. It was a disaster at first. I didn't even know what department to ask for. Marketing, I guess, but we weren't sure. We'd call whatever number looked promising. "Who is this?" "What do you want?" "Is this a crank call?" Click. We got nowhere—fast.

Meanwhile, we were looking at what we needed just to get started: a tent, stove, equipment, basic camping gear. It really was camping on the water, in our minds. We figured we needed about $1,000 just for the basics. And that didn't even include a boat. Music was at the top of the list too. We knew we needed music. So while all this was going on, I started taping cassette after cassette—probably eighty of them—from my albums. Old record player, record to cassette, label, repeat. It took me about a week, and I was doing that before we even had a concrete way to leave.

Day #1 of pitching: total flop. Day #2: We tried Caesars, another flop. The end of the summer was closing in on us, and we still didn't have a sponsor, didn't have a real plan, and still didn't have a boat. I started wavering. Kelly stayed the optimist. "It's okay, Dan," he'd say. "We'll figure it out." I wasn't so sure.

Then we called Bally's.

Beach view, Atlantic City, NJ

Chapter 2 - Are you Ready?

The Bally's call started like the others. I introduced myself as a lifeguard, said we were trying to promote Atlantic City and the casinos by rowing a lifeguard boat down to Florida, and asked if we could speak to someone who might be interested. I probably didn't even sound as coherent as that.

"Hold on one second," the woman on the phone said. I remember cupping my hand over the receiver and looking at Kelly. What's going on? In the old days, you could hear that dead space on the line and feel your heart rate climb. Then she came back on. "I'm going to put you through to our executive office." I could hardly process that. Executive office? Whose office? That's how we ended up connected to the office of a man named Billy Weinberger. We had no idea who he was at the time.

Later, I found out about his reputation. He was known nationally as the Dean of Casino Gaming—President of Caesar's Palace, then of Bally's—an international humanitarian who supported civic and religious causes. Steve Wynn once said that if you measured a man by the respect he earned from the people whose lives he touched, Billy came out as one of the most successful human beings he'd ever known. That's whose secretary I was talking to. She asked what we were thinking about, and I gave the pitch again—probably clunky but honest.

And then she said, "Can I schedule an appointment for you with Mr. Weinberger? Thursday at 11:30 a.m.?" I was stunned. I wrote everything down mechanically, not believing what I was hearing. Kelly looked at me like he wasn't even sure he'd heard me right. We had an appointment at Bally's. To us, that meant: We're in. This is it. We're golden.

Thursday came. We didn't tell Kelly's father. If he'd known, he probably would have told us we were out of our minds and shut it down. We had no suits. No fancy clothes. We went in wearing what we had—t-shirts, lifeguard shorts, sneakers. That's just who we were. On the way over, Kelly suddenly balked.

"I'm not going up there," he said. "I can't do it."

"What are you talking about," I said. "We're a team. You're going to let me go up there alone?"

He was firm. If you knew Kelly, you'd understand—there were certain things he just would not do. He could be wild and fearless in so many ways, but there were lines he wouldn't cross. This was one of them.

So there I was, in a t-shirt and shorts, walking into Bally's alone, asking people how to get to whatever floor it was. I rode the elevator up. When the doors opened, it was like stepping into a different world—thick carpet, big windows, the executive floor.

The secretary greeted me warmly and said, "You must be Dan." I think she was in on the humor of the situation. I was completely out of my element. I sat on a leather couch, sweating, sticking to it, staring at the view, feeling more and more like a fish out of water. I could feel the panic crawling up my neck.

"Mr. Weinberger will see you now," she said. I walked into a classic big-shot office—large desk, paintings, awards, neat rows of pens. It looked like something out of a movie. He sat behind the desk, calm, collected, very much at home.

"Come on in," he said. I introduced myself as best I could.

"I'm Dan Steelman. Thank you for seeing me."

"Tell me your story," he said. "What is this?" He had some notes from his secretary, and I wish I could see what she had written. Whatever it was, it got me into that room. So I started talking.

I told him we wanted to promote Atlantic City. I talked about rowing a lifeguard boat to Florida. I talked about the town, the casinos, the beaches—anything I could think of. I told him I was born in Atlantic City, and that my grandparents had a hotel called the Penn Atlantic in town. I threw every card I had on the table. While I was talking, he opened a large checkbook and began writing. I saw it out of the corner of my eye but didn't really process what was happening.

Finally, he tore out the check and slid it across the desk to me. I looked down. It was for $2,500. My brain short-circuited. I went right into babble mode, promising everything. "We'll do everything for Bally's. We'll promote you everywhere. We'll put your name on the boat. We'll . . ."

He held up a hand and stopped me. "I don't want you to promote Bally's," he said. At first, I didn't understand. That's what we'd come for. But he kept going. "Your story is intriguing to me," he said. "It feels authentic." He must have heard that I was speaking from my heart, not from some slick, polished pitch. He told me the money wasn't for advertising. He wasn't buying space on our boat or making us into billboards. "I'm giving you this," he said, "and I only want one thing from you." Anything, I thought. I would have agreed to anything at that moment. "I want you to be gentlemen," he said. "I want you to respect what you're doing and where you're going. Prepare the best you can. Do the right thing."

That was it. He wished me good luck, handed me the check, and told me I could go. I walked out in a daze, down the elevator, through the lobby, staring at the check. I'd never held that much money in my hands at one time in my life. I went outside and found Kelly, who had been circling in the car. "I got twenty-five hundred bucks," I told him. He didn't believe me. "Come on," I said. "Look. This is real. This is our start. We're going." He stared at the check, still half in disbelief.

"But we don't have a boat," he said. He wasn't wrong. But now the dream started to snowball.

We went home. My mother was floored. "Where did you get this check?" she demanded.

"From Bally's," I told her. "I went up there. I talked to the guy." Every answer was some version of, "Yeah, I did that. I don't really know how, but I did." The best reaction was from Kelly's father, Mr. O'Neill, who was a well-known businessman in Atlantic City. When he heard the name—Billy Weinberger—his jaw almost hit the floor.

"Who?" he said.

"Yeah," I told him. "He was really nice. Big-shot guy." He couldn't believe we'd gotten in to see him, let alone that he'd given us a check.

That's when things shifted. The parents started to realize we were serious, and suddenly their help began to show up. Mr. O'Neill made some calls. Before long, we had what we needed most: a boat. We got Old #10, a working fiberglass lifeguard boat. Light compared to the old wooden ones, built for the surf, built to be rowed hard. We still needed everything else—gear, food, tent—but now we had a hull to sit in, a way to move. I already had oars; so did Kelly. If you rowed at all back then, you had your own oars, the way a guitarist has his own guitar. My father loved rowing so much that we also had an old lifeguard boat at home, patched a thousand times, that lifeguards would borrow to practice. He loved that—seeing them in the boat, talking about his own lifeguard days in the late 1940s. And now, here we were, getting ready to take a lifeguard boat and row it to Florida. He couldn't believe it. But he loved it.

With the boat secured, we started to look more seriously at the path ahead. Were we going to go straight down the ocean? Or were we going to follow the Intracoastal Waterway, where the water was calmer? With the amount of equipment we planned to carry—tent, stove, bedding, food, tapes, a boom box—we couldn't risk going in and out through the surf every day. The ocean was too unpredictable. So we decided to try to stay inside, as much as possible, in bays and channels and the Intracoastal.

The problem was Delaware Bay. The official Intracoastal route takes you way up and around—up the Delaware River, then back down the Chesapeake. Motorboats can do that. We weren't going to row a hundred miles up the Delaware just to come back two hundred miles down. We pored over paper charts, looking for back bays, hidden cuts, any way through Delaware that didn't involve going all the way around. We didn't have GPS. We just had maps and local knowledge and our own common sense. We decided we would cut through the back bays wherever we could, even if it meant getting out and dragging the boat in shallow water.

We also started asking "Has anyone ever done this?" We heard about a couple of lifeguards who had rowed from Florida up to somewhere around our area, maybe during the Bicentennial. They had support boats and a whole crew. We tracked one of the guys down, and I talked to him on the phone.

"How did you manage it?" I asked. He told me about their team, the way they'd leapfrog up the coast with support. It was a different kind of operation. They were serious oarsmen, racers. I could row, and Kelly could row, but I'd always used boats more for what I loved—fishing, catching waves, messing around in the surf—than for competition or training. We didn't practice once for this trip. Not once. We rowed together that summer, sure, but not with some training schedule or mileage plan. We weren't rocket scientists. Ignorance really was bliss in this case.

By late September, the summer season was almost over. We kept working as long as we could to save money. From Bally's, we still had about $1,500 left after buying our basic gear—a tent, blow-up beds, a Coleman stove, the boom box, the Tupperware full of cassettes. We set a rough departure window and let it be known—we were actually doing this. Word spread.

One of the local Atlantic City personalities, Pinky Kravitz, picked up the story. Pinky was a well-known radio host in Atlantic City, and he gave us a spot on his show. He knew my grandparents, knew my family.

Everybody knew Pinky. We went on his show and told the story. People loved it. We went on again a second time, by popular demand. Callers phoned in asking, "When are those kids leaving?" We were local celebrities before we ever took a stroke.

All this time, I was also watching the bigger picture. I could feel a theme beginning to form, even if I couldn't name it yet. People wanted us to succeed. They didn't just cheer for us; they invested in us—time, money, attention. And in giving to us, they were getting something themselves: a story to follow, a feeling to root for.

As our departure date neared, another detail came up: our appearance. By then, we looked a little scraggly—end-of-summer hair, sun-beaten faces. We knew we'd be heading south through places where, in those days, a couple of young northern kids with long hair might not get the warmest reception, especially on the back waters or in small towns. So we cut our hair very short. On top of that, Kelly's parents knew some folks who owned a big paint franchise, MAB Paint—"Making America Beautiful." That summer they had a promotion with that slogan, and we ended up with a bunch of t-shirts that said Making America Beautiful across the front. Now picture it: two freshly shaved, all-American-looking kids in "Making America Beautiful" shirts, rowing a lifeguard boat to Florida. We looked like a patriotic ad campaign.

A friend of mine, Max, who was a commercial artist, drew a cartoon of us with an oar running through both our heads. He called us The Blister Brothers, assuming we were going to have blisters on top of blisters. We had t-shirts made by a local—Charlie the Shirt Man, with that design too. Everybody was getting in on the story. It felt like the whole town was giving us a push.

Finally, the day came. It wasn't a giant fanfare, but it was enough. The Press of Atlantic City came. Our close friends were there. My mom and dad, my grandmother, Kelly's family, people from the beach. We loaded our gear into Old #10—tent, blow-up beds, stove, cooler, tapes, boom box—and pushed off. All that talking, all that dreaming, all those phone calls and late-night plans—it all narrowed down to two guys in a boat, rowing out of Longport, NJ. The adventure had officially begun.

The adrenaline carried us through the first few miles. It felt surreal. We were doing it. Day one. Then the wind shifted. It started blowing hard out of the south, right in our faces. The current turned against us too. All day, we rowed into the wind and against the tide. Stroke after stroke, the boat creeping forward, then slipping back, forward, back. By late afternoon, we were worn out. My arms and back burned. We hadn't gotten nearly as far as we'd imagined we would. Maybe training for this trip wouldn't have been such a bad idea after all. We made it as far as Sea Isle City, NJ. That was it for day one. We were dragging, mentally and physically. The romantic image of two heroic oarsmen flying down the coast had been replaced by the reality of us grinding into wind and current, barely making headway.

We were rowing past houses along the bay when a man on his dock called out to us. "Hey, you guys! Where you heading?"

We told him the truth. "We don't know. It's our first day." He had heard about us—maybe on the radio, maybe word of mouth.

"Pull in here," he said. "Tie up at my dock."

We did. He told us he'd converted his garage into a little apartment—laundry area, a couple of beds—for summer guests. The summer season was over, and the place was empty. "Stay here tonight," he said. "No heat, but the beds are yours."

He didn't know us. We didn't know him. He just opened his place to us. That was our first night. If it weren't for him, we probably would've slept in the boat—or not slept at all. I remember lying there that night, exhausted, laughing with Kelly about how we had only made it to Sea Isle and how insane we'd been to think we'd reach Maryland in a day. The gloom lifted, replaced by a sense of realism and gratitude.

Day two, we pushed on toward Cape May. The weather turned nasty. Rain, wind, gray skies. My parents had close friends—the Trucksess's—who were like extended family. We had grown up with their daughters; our families vacationed together. They had a second home in Cape May, near the harbor. This was before cell phones. To reach anyone, you had to get to shore and find a pay phone and that's exactly what we did. They enthusiastically gave their blessing and allowed us to stay at their place. We pulled the boat up on the bank in Cape May Harbor, anchored it, and then walked almost straight across the road to the house, which overlooked the harbor.

The next day, it poured—so hard we couldn't go anywhere. We ended up spending the whole day inside, watching TV, hanging out on the couch, laughing about how we'd packed a tent and were already staying indoors like kings. We joked, "Who needs a tent?" But looming over us was the next big challenge: crossing Delaware Bay. We had never done anything like that. Twelve to fifteen miles of open water, no land in sight for most of it. No GPS. Just charts, compasses, and what Kelly's father had taught us. Before we left, he had shown us how to plot a course and told us, "You must trust this compass."

The morning we crossed was beautiful—clear skies, calm water, ideal. Still, standing at the mouth of the bay and looking out at water and sky with no visible destination was intimidating. We plotted the course as best we could to hit Lewes, Delaware. It turned out our line was almost the same as the ferry's. We launched and started rowing, feeling that mix of nerves and determination. To keep each other in check, we kept talking. "What do you think?" "I don't know. What do you think?" We followed the compass. As we got farther out, the channel that the ferry uses joined our path. The ferries passed us, blasting their horns, people leaning over the rails, waving and cheering. It was a strange feeling—tiny in our little lifeguard boat but part of something bigger. Eventually, Lewes came into view. We'd made it. We rowed into the harbor, relieved and riding a high.

Before long, another man waved us over. "Hey, you guys! Tie up over here."

He had seen us come in on a lifeguard boat or heard about what we were doing or both. He had a boat in a small marina there and offered us a place to stay on it. Again—no prior connection. Just someone impressed enough by what we were trying to do that he opened his floating home to us. By that point, I was starting to feel something I couldn't quite explain yet. What is this, I kept asking myself. Is it the time we're living in? Is it something about water people? Is it just human beings recognizing a kind of courage or craziness they relate to? I wasn't "saved" yet, not in the way I'd later come to understand faith. But even then, I started to think, this can't just be random. These people felt drawn to us. They wanted to help, and they were doing it in very concrete ways—beds, roofs, meals, safe harbors. If the trip had ended right there, in Lewes, it still would have been an amazing story. But we were just getting started.

By then, we had established a nightly routine that became a kind of glue for the whole journey. I had a little tape recorder, and every night I'd record what we'd done that day—where we started, where we ended, who we met, and what we learned. I also kept a written log, day by day, e.g. Day One. Day Two. Crossing Delaware Bay. The man in Sea Isle. The Trucksess's house. The boat in Lewes. I did it religiously, every single day. We'd eat, talk about the day, and then either I'd write or we spoke into the recorder, capturing it while it was still fresh. It served as therapy as much as record-keeping. It helped us process what we experienced and kept us grounded in the reality of what we were doing.

From Delaware, we started looking south again. The Intracoastal proper didn't really help us where we were, so we had to "wing it" a bit—finding our own way through bays and cuts, talking to local boaters, asking which markers to keep on our right or left, what to look for. Locals were always generous with information. "If you see that point, go this way." "Keep those pilings on your starboard side." That kind of thing. We pressed on, sometimes rowing in water so shallow we had to get out and drag the boat for long stretches. There's a photo in my mind of us trudging through skinny water, pulling Old #10, laughing about our "shortcuts." We stayed with more people—older couples who let us into their homes, folks who owned boats and put us up on board, people who had converted garages and little sheds. Always the same pattern: strangers offering what they had.

Eventually we made it to Ocean City, Maryland. We decided to stop there for a night, rest, get our bearings, resupply, and behave like the slightly immature young guys we were. We had about $1,500 left from Bally's, so we splurged—got a cheap hotel room, wandered around, and soaked in the scene. We pulled our boat up, left it where we could keep an eye on it, and took a breather.

The press was starting to catch on more regularly by then. I can't even remember how some of the reporters found us. Maybe they saw the boat and our shirts, maybe someone tipped them off. They'd come down to the dock, snap a few pictures, and ask what we were doing. At first, we stuck with the "promoting Atlantic City" story. But the more we talked, the more bored I got with that angle. After all, Billy Weinberger had told us flat-out—he didn't want or need the promotion. So, one day, half as a joke, we shifted our story. "We're rowing to help save the whales." We thought it was funny—two kids in a lifeguard boat, "promoting whales." In different towns, we tried different causes. In one article we were promoting Atlantic City. In another, saving the whales. Later on, I think in South Carolina, we picked up some other cause entirely. Underneath the joking, though, we were serious about the rowing.

From Maryland, we kept going—and we started to notice something new: the boating community itself. People were moving their boats south for the winter. Others were young folks living on small sailboats, working in coastal towns during the summer, then sailing down to Florida to pick up odd jobs—waiting tables, bartending, whatever they could find. They'd stay a while, then move on to the next town. We would meet them in marinas and along the waterways. They would hear about us, or see us, or someone would point at us and say, "Those are the guys rowing to Florida." We also began to notice that we kept running into the same people.

There was one wild guy in a little beat-up motorboat. He wore goggles and blasted past us now and then, waving as he disappeared into the distance. Later we would catch up to him and find him high and dry up on a sandbar, working on his engine. There were three guys from New York in a small sailboat. We called them "The Dudes." They were headed to Florida too. We saw them over and over again, leapfrogging each other up and down the coast as currents, tides, and mechanical issues mixed up everybody's pace.

By then, we were calling into the Pinky Kravitz show once a week from pay phones, giving updates. People in Atlantic City were following our progress. "Where are those guys now?" they'd ask. One night, we were hanging out with The Dudes on their boat—five of us, drinking a few beers, laughing and feeling good. I had the bright idea to call Pinky's show live. We didn't have a phone, but The Dudes had a ship-to-shore radio. In those days, if you wanted to call land from a boat, you called the marine operator, who would patch you through to a regular phone line. It was expensive, but we didn't think about that part. We called the radio station ship-to-shore, and they accepted the call. We were hooting and hollering, banging on the boat, singing, just being loud, foolish, young guys. Pinky wasn't ready for that kind of chaos on a live show, and I'm certain he didn't know how much that call was costing the station. We were probably on for twenty minutes before he'd had enough and cut us off. After that, he never took a live call from us again. People later gave him some grief about it—"Whatever happened to those guys?"—but I don't blame him. He had no idea what he was getting into that night.

By that time, we were deep into the rhythm of the trip. We weren't fighting; in fact we almost never argued. I think that's part of why Kelly and I made such a good team. We could spend hours together in a boat, talk about anything, and still get up the next day and do it again. We kept moving south.

Our family support team for the send-off

The local crowd getting into the action

Kelly and I wondering out loud what we got ourselves into
Photo by *The Press* of Atlantic City

First couple of strokes of many to come
Photo by *The Press* of Atlantic City

Pushing and pulling our way
through the backwaters of Delaware

Chapter 3 - Southern Fried Strokes

Somewhere along the way—before North Carolina fully opened up in front of us—we reached one of the biggest milestones of the trip: The Chesapeake Bay. We had worked our way down to the area of the Chesapeake Bay Bridge. It was daunting—this huge body of water, big shipping lanes, fast currents, the whole thing. Right around that time, it was Kelly's birthday. That morning, before the crossing, we celebrated as best we could out on the water. Nothing fancy—just the two of us in a lifeguard boat, marking the day. Then we set out to row across.

If you've ever driven over the Chesapeake Bay Bridge, you know how long it is. From the water, it feels even longer. We had to row about twenty miles across the bay and then continue on to position ourselves near Norfolk so we could get into the Dismal Swamp Canal. On top of the distance, there were currents to deal with and big ships—naval vessels and container ships—moving through the shipping lanes. We charted our course and pushed off. It turned into the hardest day of the entire trip. We rowed for roughly eighteen hours. Across the Chesapeake, then up toward Norfolk. By the time we finally found an old cheap hotel right on the water with a dock, we were done. Completely done. We pulled in, tied up, and dragged ourselves inside. My hands had locked into claws; I couldn't straighten my fingers. I had to soak them in buckets of ice just to get some movement back.

We stayed there that night and another day, recovering. After that, we pushed on up toward Norfolk to catch the entrance to the Dismal Swamp Canal. To get into the canal, we had to go through a series of locks. For two kids from the Jersey shore, locks were fascinating. You row into this concrete chamber with all these other boats, the gates close behind you, and the water either fills or drains to raise or lower you to the level of the next stretch of water.

The Dismal Swamp Canal itself—if I remember correctly—was either engineered or strongly advocated by George Washington. It's a long, straight cut through the swamp, calm and quiet. After the chaos of the Chesapeake, it felt like glass. We saw deer swimming across the canal, their heads cutting little V-shaped wakes in the still water. The air felt different there—heavy but peaceful. We ran into The Dudes again in the canal. Their small sailboat couldn't really sail in that narrow cut, and their engine wasn't big, so we could keep pace with them easily. We hung out with them through parts of the swamp, talking, drifting, enjoying the ease of the water. For us, the canal was a gift—a long, calm reprieve after an eighteen-hour grind across an open bay. When I look back now, the Chesapeake still stands out as one of the toughest physical challenges I've ever faced. But what I remember just as strongly is what came after: the stillness of the canal, the deer, the slow movement forward, the simple relief of being carried along in smooth water. It was another lesson the trip kept teaching us over and over: Storms, then calm. Hard days, then unexpected kindness. Big crossings, then quiet canals. And somewhere in all of that, two kids in a lifeguard boat kept going south, stroke by stroke, night after night, writing it all down as we went.

We called this the second half. The part of the journey that started after the Chesapeake and the Dismal Swamp. The point where we weren't just making it—we were becoming something else. One boat. One rhythm. One flow. The southern half of the trip came with a new kind of energy. Our confidence was growing—not from arrogance but from experience. Kelly and I were syncing up. Solving problems without talking, reading the weather, and adjusting mid-stroke. He had always been the water guy—surfer, boater, salt in his blood. I came into it late. But now, I could feel myself tuning in. We were starting to row like a team that didn't need to speak, we just knew.

After we passed through the Dismal Swamp Canal, it was as if the water itself was giving us permission, almost like we had leveled up. And strangely, other boaters had started hearing about us—two young guys, rowing to Florida. Rumors were moving faster than we were. People were starting to look for us, expect us. That was surreal. Then came the night in Elizabeth City. We found a little public dock and set up for the night. Not long after, our friends from the New York sailboat crew pulled in beside us. It felt safe. We all piled into their vessel, joking and talking, making soup or peanut butter sandwiches, the usual. Then the boat rocked. A figure stood in the doorway, uninvited. Behind him—figures in the dark. We froze. Nobody climbs aboard without asking. Tension filled the cabin, then Kelly stood up slowly. He didn't say a word, he just lifted his sweatshirt, and there it was: a gun tucked into his waistband. The message was clear. The intruders got the hint and backed off without a word, then vanished into the night.

The adrenaline didn't fade for hours. As we rowed away in the dark—three or four miles in silence—we knew we'd dodged something big. That was the closest we ever came to real danger. I turned to Kelly in disbelief: "You were gonna tell me about the gun . . . when?"

He shrugged and said, "Didn't think it was necessary." In hindsight, I was glad he had it and glad he didn't say anything until it mattered. But man—that moment changed things. From there, the trip turned quieter, deeper.

The stretch of North Carolina we were in was wild and undeveloped. Swamps, tangles of trees, no real towns. Just the sound of water and wind. We started rowing at night, following the tides by feel. We didn't have tide charts, but somehow—we just knew. How strange and beautiful it was to feel yourself becoming part of something greater. The pull of the tide, the sound of the water, and the life all around it seemed to carry a quiet meaning beyond themselves. Sight, sound, and movement were heightened, as if something unseen was stirring just beneath the surface. In that moment, it felt as though every current, every breeze, every whisper of the shore was gently reminding you that you were not alone.

One night, I woke up in the tent and whispered, "You awake?"

Kelly answered, "Yeah."

Then at the same time we both said, "It's time to row." That's when I knew we were entering some kind of flow state. It wasn't just rowing anymore, it was rhythm, timing and intuition. It was spiritual.

We floated through channels lit with nets and lanterns

like a floating Christmas parade. Fishermen were catching "spot," a type of small fish, at night and their lights made the water shimmer in the dark. And then came the dolphins. We heard them before we saw them—breathing alongside us, gliding through the water. Sometimes they nudged the boat gently, like they were playing or guiding or blessing. It was real. It happened. And it blew my mind. Then one night, something else came through the dark: a barge. We couldn't see it until it was almost on top of us. Full speed, no warning and massive. We barely made it to the edge of the channel in time. The wake nearly capsized us. The pull of water, the pounding noise—it was chaos. And just like that, it was gone, into the night. We sat there, shaken, alive. I remember thinking, "How do we keep surviving this?" I didn't know, but I started to believe something bigger watched over us. We didn't get much rain on that trip; somehow, the weather was mostly clear. That was another gift. Looking back now, I know—those weren't coincidences. They were compass points of grace, guiding us forward, one stroke at a time.

After all that had happened, I realized I needed to rewind—mentally and spiritually—back to where we were just after the Elizabeth City incident. We entered a stretch of the journey where things felt aligned. We were one with the boat; confident, committed, campers of the river, explorers of brackish waters. We followed rivers with names that sounded like stories—the Neuse River, the Alligator River. The Neuse was long and peaceful, full of wildlife and warm light. The Alligator, on the other hand, lived up to its name, wild, remote and oddly, shared with a military zone. As we rowed across its glassy surface, military jets strafed the air overhead, tearing across the sky like thunder gods, and the mosquitoes seemed to be doing the same thing. It was chaos and beauty combined. We laughed as we read signs on the shore: Do Not Anchor—Military Zone. There we were, floating past an artillery testing range, saluting to imaginary generals. It was bizarre and completely unforgettable.

From there we crossed into Myrtle Beach, South Carolina. We were back in civilization, or something like it. More boats. More waves. More strangers recognizing us. "You're the rowboat guys, right?" one shouted. Then a generous offer: "Come stay at my place a few miles up." We accepted gratefully, but navigating Myrtle Beach wasn't like navigating rivers. It was street after street, cul-de-sac after cul-de-sac. Darkness fell and then the rain came. The guy's directions, generous as they were, didn't help much without a map or phone. We spent hours trying to find his house. Soaked and exhausted, we ended up back in the tent by the boat. Still, the offer reminded me: people were good. Even if it didn't work out, his kindness counted.

A few days later, we reached Wrightsville Beach, NC. It was picture-perfect. Blue skies. Boats docked along the marina and people waved as we rowed by. We found a spot beside a high concrete wall near a clean, local marina. That evening, as Kelly slept in the boat, I laid out on the dock, just taking it all in. The kind of peace that only comes when the water is calm and the air is still. That's when she showed up. A woman on a bicycle, probably in her fifties.

She looked over the wall and asked, "Are you the boys going to Miami?"

I nodded. "Yeah, that's us."

"I brought this for you," she said. She handed me a full bag of groceries, just like that. No explanation. No expectation. Just, "You remind me of my son." And she pedaled away. I was stunned. Still am.

The bag was packed with perfect things—cookies,

snacks, and drinks. The kind of things a mom would pack. I opened the cooler and started unloading, and suddenly the tears came. Not because I was sad but because I was overwhelmed. This was what the trip was becoming: not just an adventure but grace in human form. We didn't know her name. We never saw her again. But her gesture became a cornerstone in my memory, something sacred. That's what the water had taught me so far—that every stroke might lead to a storm, a stranger, or a moment that would change you forever.

By now, the boating world knew us. People looked out for us. At the small marinas where we stopped, the owners would say things like, "You're the rowboat guys, right? Yeah, we heard about you. Showers are over there. Stay as long as you like." That kindness—it wasn't just appreciated; it was fuel. We weren't chasing records, and we weren't out to impress anyone. But people still clapped when we arrived, not because we were heroes—but because they saw something in us; maybe determination, maybe wonder, or maybe just two young guys trying something bigger than themselves.

And then we arrived in Charleston. Neither of us knew what to expect of Charleston before we got there; we were just following our mileage. But when we pulled in that evening, the city felt . . . different; old, warm, a real southern charm to it. I needed to do laundry, so I left Kelly to explore while I tackled the laundromat blues. That's where I met her. She walked in like she belonged—because she did. A local college student with a sharp wit and kind eyes.

I asked, awkwardly, "Do you live here?"

She laughed, "What do you think I'm doing at a laundromat?"

Fair enough. We started talking, and she began to

tell me about Charleston—its history, its soul, the college scene. She loved it there, and the more we talked, the more she opened up. I asked if she'd show us around, and she agreed even though she hadn't met Kelly yet. When Kelly arrived, I introduced them. She looked at Kelly—tall, calm, naturally athletic—and then back at me. Most girls we met said I reminded them of their little brother, I was used to it. But this wasn't about romance; this was about connection. She took us out that night to a local hangout, low-key, comfortable, and full of life. When we said we'd just camp on the dock, she insisted, "You're staying with me."

Her apartment was one big high-ceilinged room with just a bed in one corner, a small kitchen off to the side, and enough space for two sleeping bags. We stayed for two or three days, and she showed us the city, gave us rest, and treated us like family. It's always the strangers who become part of your story.

We said goodbye with full hearts and moved on, only to be greeted again—less than an hour down the waterway—by another stranger. A young guy ran out, "You're the guys, right?" He'd heard about us too. His dad was a boater. They probably would've housed us too, if we'd asked. And on we went.

Another highlight: Kelly's dad flew down to meet us. He literally flew into a random coastal town just to visit. That meant everything. A shot of encouragement. A reminder that people were cheering us on. All of it—the strangers, the hosts, the dolphins, the near misses—was shaping something in us. This wasn't just an adventure anymore. It was a pilgrimage, a sacred unfolding. We didn't have a tourist guide. We didn't pick stops for their beauty. We just . . . arrived. Wherever the tide took us. And it took us to grace, again and again.

Finding things of interest on the way wasn't hard

View of our friends "The Dudes" vessel from our camp site somewhere along the Virginia shoreline

Heading out of the Chesapeake Bay
toward the locks of the Dismal Swamp Canal

Patiently waiting in the lock system of the Dismal Swamp Canal

Our seemingly endless view of the Dismal Swamp Canal

Taking a break from the morning row

View from campsite in the Albemarle Sound, North Carolina

Chapter 4 - A Parish, a Priest, and a New Beginning

Charleston was now behind us, and our sights were set on Hilton Head. I had history there—family friends, warm memories from younger years. We pulled in without a plan as usual, and tied up at a dock surrounded by yachts so clean they looked like they had never known salt or trouble or hunger. We started asking around: "Where could we stay?"

A hotel manager overheard us and said, "I know who you are—you're the rowboat guys. I've got a room for you through the weekend—no charge." Not only that, he called up *The Islander* magazine. "They need to tell your story," he said. It was surreal. One minute, you're rowing into town looking like castaways, the next, you're doing a photo shoot for a glossy coastal magazine. That transition made it feel unreal, like a tide change you don't notice until the current has already turned. But I had my own plan brewing too. I called my buddy Rick, a student at Clemson University.

"I'm in Hilton Head," I told him. "Can you pick me up?"

He said yes. I didn't tell Kelly. I should have, but I was so excited to see a familiar face and escape for a couple of days, just to step out of the journey for a moment. I figured Kelly had the hotel, the boat was safe, and it would all be fine.

Clemson was wild. Youth. Noise. Parties. It was sensory overload after weeks of quiet water. I loved it, but I forgot where I was supposed to be. I forgot who I was supposed to be loyal to. When I got back, everything seemed okay—until I asked Kelly for the cassette tapes, the spoken record of the trip. Gone. He had taped over them—with music from the radio. I was stunned. All our recorded memories, erased.

"I got lonely," he said. And that was all he needed to say. I'd left him. He was alone in a town we didn't know, surrounded by strangers, and I had gone off chasing a good time. I felt about two inches tall. But Kelly didn't blame me. He forgave me, quietly, completely. And that's how I knew—again—he was the only person I could have done this with. We pressed on.

We reached Savannah, Georgia. That morning, we pulled up onto a beach—one of the only times we got close to the open coast due to the fact that we usually stayed on the Intracoastal Waterway. It looked safe enough, which should have been the first warning. We hauled the boat above the tide line, anchored it, and left our gear aboard. Two young park rangers who lived nearby offered us a place to crash, so we accepted. That night, a storm hit. A real one. Wind, rain, waves slamming against the seawall. It roared for hours. We could barely sleep. By morning, the storm had passed—and so had everything in our boat. The vessel sat there, half-buried in sand, like a relic from a failed civilization, completely empty. No duffel bags. No food. No gear. No oars. Nothing. We sat on the beach in silence. Just two guys in soaked t-shirts and shorts, staring at the wreckage of our journey.

"This is it," I said. "It's over." We were broken, devastated, already rehearsing what we'd tell our parents. Kelly was quiet, but his eyes burned with stubborn hope.

Then, through the fog, a figure appeared. A man in black with a white collar, smoking a pipe, walking straight toward us like something out of a black-and-white film. At first, I thought it was Bing Crosby from the movie *The Bells of St. Mary's* or maybe Pat O'Brien from *Angels with Dirty Faces*.

"Morning, boys," he said. "What's the problem?" We explained, barely able to talk. He didn't say much, then just turned toward the ocean and pointed. "What's that?"

Floating along with the current and tide—our duffel bag. We ran into the water hauled in our waterlogged duffle bag. "What about those?" he asked. Our oars followed! One by one bopping in like obedient soldiers. Only our spare oars were taken by the storm. He nodded, puffed his pipe, and said, "Let's get you cleaned up."

Turns out, he was a Catholic priest—Father Tom from St. Michael's Parish. He brought down a wagon, loaded us up, and took us to the church. Fed us. Helped us wash everything. Gave us two days to regroup. We lost our logbook in the storm, but somehow, gained a deeper story. The moment I thought it was over turned out to be a resurrection. A literal fog-lifting, spirit-saving, grace-drenched miracle. What should have been the end became a new beginning. And once again, the water carried us forward.

It was strange how we found ourselves there—at the parish, of all places. Not because we planned it and not because we made any smart move that got us there. It was almost comical, like beginner's luck on a divine scale. Somehow, we had landed in the care of a Catholic priest who saw to all our needs—food, shelter, guidance, even laughter. We didn't seek it out, and yet, there we were. Every detail felt orchestrated by something—or Someone—beyond our control. It was too perfect to explain. I had to laugh at how this trip kept unfolding, as if heaven itself had taken the helm. I couldn't have dreamed it up if I tried. This wasn't a dream—it was the dream come true. That time at the parish gave us a chance to regroup and reenergize. Gratitude became the air we breathed. After so much loss and uncertainty, it felt good to have our feet on solid ground again.

The day was busy—washing, cleaning, readying the boat for what came next. We got the laundry done, dried out what we could, and made sure every bit of usable gear had a purpose. The only real problem was our cooking setup. Our old Coleman stove—the one that had survived so many campsites—was totaled. It had been buried in sand and saltwater, and there was no saving it. We figured we'd just build fires as we went, like we had before. But Father Tom must have overheard our conversation. Just before we left, he appeared quietly with a new stove in his hands. He mentioned they had an extra one lying around. I'm sure that wasn't true—it was a gift, and we both knew it. He didn't say much, never made a big show of anything. That was his way—calm, grounded, steady. He had a way of making you feel seen without needing to say much at all. His words carried weight, and though he spoke from his faith, it never felt heavy-handed. At the time, I didn't think of myself as particularly religious, but I knew something deeper was happening. Looking back now, I can see it clearly—he wasn't just helping us fix a stove or get back on the water; he was helping us find direction again.

Somewhere between loads of laundry and tightening lines, we ran into one of the rangers—the very same man who'd offered us his home when we needed it most. He stopped by just to check on us, to make sure we were still afloat, in more ways than one. When he heard we hoped to move on soon, he offered to drive us into Savannah. That simple kindness felt like another blessing. Father Tom, the priest, knew the ranger and gave his quiet nod of approval, his gentle blessing to go. That night, another local friend took us out into the city. And for the first time in a long while, we were able to enjoy it. No black cloud hanging overhead, no worries about the next meal or the next storm. Just the lights of Savannah, the laughter, the relief of surviving the hard parts. It was the cherry on top after everything we'd endured.

By the time we turned in, our minds were racing again—excited, ready, curious. We had our charts spread out on the table, not all of them but enough to see that we were standing on the edge of something big. Georgia seemed like it was nearly behind us—Florida lay ahead. The thought of crossing that line felt monumental, like we were entering a new chapter of the same dream. Every state before had its challenges, but Florida symbolized something different—warmth, hope, and maybe even the finish line.

We talked about routes: should we stay in the Intracoastal or weave through the islands? The islands called to us. They looked faster, freer, wilder. We could see the wildlife and feel the pulse of creation again. We decided—we'd take the road less traveled, even if it wasn't really a road at all. We would head out into the ocean—straight through the surf, with an extra three or four hundred pounds of gear loaded into the boat. Probably not the smartest idea, but that's how we operated back then: bold, a little reckless, and completely caught up in the adventure. Little did we know, of course, that the remainder of Georgia and Florida had its own lessons waiting for us. Looking back, that stretch through Georgia turned out to be one of the coolest, most unforgettable parts of the entire journey.

The day finally came when Father Tom, with that gentle firmness of his, kicked us out of the nest. We had everything packed, cleaned, and ready to go. The boat was solid again, the gear stowed neatly, our spirits high. Gratitude had replaced anxiety. After everything we'd been through, it felt good to move forward with clear skies and calm hearts. We said our goodbyes, thanked him once more. With his quiet blessing and that brand-new stove packed onboard, we pushed off again. True to form, we didn't take the safe route. We took the unconservative approach, the one that promised more risk—and more discovery. And once again, we felt that invisible hand guiding us forward.

The ocean stretched out calm and glassy that morning—a good omen if ever there was one. We slipped back into rhythm, the oars cutting clean through the water, the salt wind brushing against our faces. It felt right. It felt like we were back. For the first time in a long time, there was no heaviness over us. The black cloud that had followed us through storms and setbacks had lifted. Florida was somewhere ahead, and even though we couldn't see it yet, we could feel it calling us. The one thing we hadn't lost through it all was our music. The music blasted down the coast like a victory cry. You probably could've heard it echoing down the coast for miles—our little floating jukebox roaring with rock and roll. It was loud, messy, joyful, and absolutely necessary. It was our soundtrack to freedom, and that morning, the beat was back.

Even years later, Father Tom stuck with us. When my wife Terry and I recently visited Kelly and his wife Laurie down in the Keys, I asked him if he remembered the priest's name. He didn't even hesitate. "Yeah," he said, "Father Tom." That simple memory hit me harder than I expected. We hadn't talked much about that time, but it was clear that Father Tom had left an imprint on both of us. Some people enter a journey briefly and leave changed. Others enter it briefly and change it instead. Father Tom was the second kind. He had shown up exactly when we needed him—not just to help but to remind us that we weren't alone on our journey.

On our way through Hilton Head we had a nice article featured in their local magazine *The Islander*

This was our typical Grade A docking slip at most of the marina overnights
Photo by: Candace Lovely / *Islander Magazine*

Father Tom showing up right on time and surveying the situation.
We actually saved Kelly's red sweatpants.

Gloomy view of the beach disaster the next morning from the Ranger's outside deck

This is what was left of the beach after the evening's storm

Chapter 5 - Wandering in the Maze

We studied the chart as we rowed, pointing out landmarks and islands we didn't recognize. The map hinted at possibilities, but we didn't really know what lay ahead, and that was part of the thrill. The farther we went, the quieter the world became. No high-rises, no boardwalks, no neon lights—just endless stretches of wild coast. It reminded us of those untouched places up in North Carolina, where civilization hadn't quite caught up yet. After several long hours of rowing, we spotted a beach that looked inviting enough to land. We didn't know it then, but we'd stumbled onto one of the barrier islands managed by the Georgia Department of Natural Resources—one of those places few people were allowed to visit. But as usual, we just sort of winged it.

We made it ashore without trouble, pulled the boat high onto the sand, and set about picking our spot for the night. As we unloaded the gear, something caught my eye—big white disks scattered across the beach. At first glance, they looked like giant pancakes, but when we bent down to look closer, we realized they were sand dollars.

They were everywhere. Dozens upon dozens, glimmering in the light. We started gathering them up, filling a plastic bag with at least twenty. It was the kind of sight that tells you you're standing somewhere untouched, a place where people don't often walk. The beach was pristine, silent, and alive. The tide whispered in and out, and the air carried that clean, salty stillness you only find in wild places. We set up our tent and started talking about where to build a fire. That's when Kelly noticed the tracks. He stopped, bent down, and called me over.

"What do you think these are?" he said. I looked down at the sand—large, rounded prints, deep and deliberate. For a moment, my imagination got the best of me.

"Lion paws," I said, half-joking, half-not. He looked at me and laughed, but the truth was, neither of us knew what we were dealing with. Whatever it was, it was big. And we were a long way from home.

A lot of those barrier islands have bobcats, though you'd never see them unless they wanted you to. But we saw the tracks—big, heavy prints sunk deep in the sand. Something wild had been there. We joked about it, of course, but deep down we both knew this wasn't housecat territory. That's when I brought up the gun again.

"Hey, Kelly," I said, "you might want to check that thing—just in case something decides to pay us a visit tonight." It was just a nervous reminder we weren't alone out there. We laughed it off, set up camp, and got the fire going. Father Tom's stove made its debut that evening, and I couldn't help smiling as we cooked our first meal on it. His quiet blessing seemed to follow us right into the wilderness.

As night fell, the beach turned magical. The stars came out one by one, filling the sky like lanterns. The ocean whispered just beyond the firelight. It was one of those perfect nights you dream about—where you sit with a friend, guitar in hand, and realize that for all the chaos and loss, somehow life has brought you here. We probably weren't supposed to build that fire—definitely not legal on protected land—but we didn't know any better. We were young, grateful, and alive. Later that night, the wilderness reminded us where we were. Strange, guttural cries echoed through the dunes, deep and wild. I lay there for a long time listening, wondering what kind of creature made that sound. Kelly didn't seem too concerned, but I couldn't shake the feeling we were visitors in someone else's home.

Morning came early. The sunrise spilled gold over the beach, and the air smelled of salt and dew. Kelly needed his coffee—he always did—so we fired up Father Tom's stove again and brewed a pot before breaking camp. As we loaded the boat, I noticed the surf starting to build. It wasn't bad yet, but we both knew enough about the ocean to recognize what was coming. The waves were stacking higher, rolling with more force. It was time to move. We looked over our charts and spotted a narrow route that could take us inland to reconnect with the Intracoastal Waterway. It wasn't close, but it was doable. So we pushed off, rowing hard through the growing surf, bouncing over waves rougher than we'd planned for. By the time we slipped into calmer waters, we were soaked but relieved.

That night, we couldn't find anything that remotely looked like a sheltered and calm place to camp, so we made the boat our home. It wasn't the first time, and it wouldn't be the last. We had figured out how to pitch our little tent right inside the boat—anchored out, oars laid across for a base, bed cushions on top, and the tent pitched snug in the middle. As long as we didn't both lean to one side, we were good. It was ridiculous, ingenious, and oddly comfortable. We slept like that more times than I can count—floating under the stars, the boat rocking gently with the tide.

By the next morning, the scenery began to change. The coastline gave way to winding channels and tall marsh grasses that seemed to go on forever. The waterways twisted and turned in every direction, each one looking just like the last. It felt like being caught inside a green maze—miles of water and reeds stretching to the horizon. The world grew quiet again. No roads, no houses, no signs of life, just the rhythmic pull of our oars and the whisper of wind across the grass. We didn't know it then, but this stretch through Georgia's wild marshlands would become one of the most hauntingly beautiful parts of the entire journey. It was raw, untouched, and humbling. Every stroke reminded us that adventure isn't always about finding something new—it's about rediscovering wonder in places most people never see.

Day after day, we kept winding through that endless labyrinth of backwaters and canals. Four days, maybe more—it all blurred together. Every turn looked like the last. Marsh grass. Muddy water. Sky. Repeat. At first, it was peaceful, even hypnotic. But as the hours turned into days, a strange unease began to creep in. I remember looking around and saying, "Man, this is bad. Where are we even?" It didn't make sense. We'd been rowing for what felt like forever, and yet nothing changed. It was like the world had folded in on itself—a green and gold carousel spinning in slow motion but never going anywhere. We started noticing what wasn't there. No houses. No docks. No boats. Just silence. Once in a while, we'd spot an oyster fisherman motoring through the distance, but even that felt like a mirage. Something was off, and we both knew it. The wind began to stir. The air, which had been warm and still, turned restless. Clouds gathered on the horizon. The weather had been so steady, we hadn't thought to check for changes—but now it was changing fast. We had no weather radio, no forecast, no plan—just music. The songs played on, hour after hour, shifting with our moods. Sometimes it kept us going. Sometimes it just made the silence more noticeable.

The channels started to open up into broad, shallow lakes. Each crossing meant another battle—rowing hard across exposed water just to find the next thin ribbon of a canal. We were tired, hungry, and frustrated. "Let's just keep going," Kelly said, and I agreed. We both knew stopping wasn't an option. By late afternoon, the sky had gone gray. The wind was rising fast, pushing against us. Then it started to get dark—too dark. We were still rowing, the marshes giving way to open water again. The waves slapped hard against the hull, and the air filled with spray.

"This isn't good," I said quietly.

We were in some kind of wide basin, maybe an inland sound, maybe something else—we didn't know. But the wind was howling now. It tore at our oars, spun the boat sideways, and drove us wherever it wanted. The rain came suddenly, like a wall. One minute we rowed blind in the wind; the next, we couldn't see our own hands in front of us. The drops hit like stones, sharp and cold. The boat lurched, twisted, and slid sideways on the chop. It was chaos—darkness, wind, water, and the constant sound of rain hammering the surface. We weren't terrified, not yet. But we were past the point of control. Concern turned to urgency. We needed to find shelter, some direction, some way out. And as the storm pushed harder, we realized the truth—whatever plan we thought we had, it was gone. The marsh, the maze, the calm—all of it had vanished. We were at the mercy of the wind again.

At some point in that chaos, we stopped fighting the wind and realized we were no longer moving at all—we'd been tossed straight up onto the marsh. The reeds were taller than the boat. The rain came in sheets, and every gust slammed us sideways. In desperation, we threw the anchor. It caught—thank God it caught—and the line held tight. We were perched half in, half out of the water, stuck in the weeds and being beaten around like a toy. The wind howled through the grass, bending it flat, rattling every nerve we had left. We scrambled to make shelter. We pulled out the tarp from our tent and tied it down to the oar thimbles, creating a makeshift cover. It didn't matter; we were soaked through anyway. All we could think about was the anchor—would it hold through the night? If it didn't, we'd be blown who-knows-where in the dark, with no way to see or steer.

Every so often, Kelly crawled out to the bow to check the line. I remember watching him disappear into the spray, holding onto the rope like it was our last thread to safety. We could feel the boat shift and strain, but the anchor held. It was a long, bumpy, sleepless night—one that seemed to stretch on forever. When morning finally came, the rain eased, though the wind was still fierce. We were cold, wet, hungry, and completely spent. There were no boats, no people, no signs of life. Just gray skies and the steady roar of the wind. That day and the next, we were trapped—stranded in the marsh, waiting for the storm to pass. It was one of the lowest points of the entire trip. The kind of moment where you question every decision that got you there. Why did we keep going? Why didn't we just stop? It wasn't fear so much as weariness; bone-deep exhaustion. Mentally, I was near the end of myself.

The wind finally began to die—still blowing fifteen, maybe twenty miles an hour, but manageable—we decided it was time. No sleep, no real food, just sheer determination. We dug our oars in and fought our way out of that marsh. Stroke by stroke, we clawed our way back into open water. When we finally reached solid ground again, we dropped anchor and stumbled ashore. Everything we owned was soaked. We pitched the tent on higher ground, wrung out what we could, and collapsed. We slept through most of that next day.

By morning, the sky was lighter. The world seemed to breathe again. We packed up, still sore and groggy, and started rowing. Slowly, the signs of life began to return—first a distant motor, then another boat, and then, finally, a fisherman close enough to hail. He looked at us like we were ghosts.

"What are you guys doing out here?" he shouted. We told him the short version—that we'd been caught in bad weather. He shook his head in disbelief. "You didn't hear? There's been a hurricane offshore—Hurricane Kendra. It's been blowing through for days!"

Kelly and I just looked at each other. It explained everything—the winds, the chaos, the eerie emptiness. We'd been rowing through the edge of a hurricane, without a clue. When he motored away, I just stared at the water and whispered, "Thank you." I didn't even know who I was talking to—God, fate, the angels, maybe all three. But I meant it. That wasn't luck. That was mercy. Once again, we'd somehow come through what should have finished us. There was no other explanation.

Someone—something—was watching over us. And as the marshlands fell behind us and the sky began to clear, I knew deep down that this journey wasn't just about endurance anymore. It was about grace.

Another day of moving on in the backwaters of Georgia. We were still damp and cold, and honestly, at that point, I was thinking more about hot showers than the beauty around us. The scenery was still there—the marshes, the sky, the birds—but it had taken a backseat to my thoughts of warmth, food, and rest. We hadn't eaten much in days. We still had a little soup left, but everything was dwindling. It had been a long, strange stretch through Georgia. When I look back, it started out beautifully—peaceful, even magical—but after that storm, things changed. We ended up wet, tired, and hungry. It was the first time on the trip we had been all three for that long. But I couldn't feel sorry for myself, not really. After all we'd been through, self-pity didn't seem fitting. When you're in a small boat and the only way out is forward, you just row and think. And what I was thinking about was Florida.

We knew it was close. Florida had become our great milestone, the goal that kept us moving. Each state was a victory, and Florida was the crown. In my head, I pictured all the things I remembered from driving there as a teenager—the sun, the palm trees, the feeling of arrival. That thought kept me going. The day itself wasn't bad, all things considered, the air was cool, the sky gray, but we had rhythm again. I was in the stern, setting the pace, Kelly was in the bow navigating. He could tell when I was starting to fade. We had rowed so many miles together that he didn't even have to say anything. If I missed a stroke, he'd "accidentally" tap me in the back with his oar—his way of keeping me alert. We kept at it, quiet and steady, until Kelly suddenly looked over his shoulder.

"What's that?" he said. "Looks weird . . . odd." Something in the water caught his attention. It broke the monotony, so as usual our curiosity won out and we steered toward it.

The closer we got, the stranger it looked. It wasn't like the usual things we'd seen floating around, and we had seen plenty of odd sights on this trip—glowing waves in Maryland, dolphins nudging our boat, even archaeologists combing through old graves that had been exposed by the tides. But this was different. As we got closer, we realized—it was a boat. A big one. Maybe over thirty feet long, but the shape was unusual. It didn't look nautical—it looked . . . well, like concrete. And that's exactly what it was—a cement boat. I'd never seen one before. Growing up around the water, I thought I'd seen it all. But a cement boat? That was new to me. Apparently, during World War II, quite a few of them were made, but this was the first time I had seen one.

We rowed closer, and two people waved to us. They were friendly—probably in their late twenties, a little older than us. The man, who I'll call Captain Mike, and his girlfriend, who was tall and kind, welcomed us aboard. They were just as curious about us as we were about them. We were cold, wet, and worn down, but they greeted us like old friends. Mike gave us the tour, proudly showing off his unusual vessel. It was slow and heavy-looking but surprisingly spacious inside. I remember thinking it probably didn't go much faster than we did rowing—but it had warmth, food, and shelter, and that was luxury to us. The galley smelled amazing. They were cooking something that made my stomach wake up for the first time in days.

They insisted we stay with them. Kelly, still wearing his red sweatpants—soaked and sagging—looked like a half-drowned rat.

The woman laughed kindly and said, "You two look like the wet rats we see swimming around these marshes." And she wasn't wrong. We all laughed together, and it felt good to laugh again.

They told us their story—how they had come all the way from Michigan in that cement boat, traveling through some route that connected the Great Lakes to the Intracoastal. I don't remember all the details, but their story fascinated me. We told them ours, and they couldn't believe it—two guys rowing this far in an open boat. They laughed at us; we laughed at them. It was one of those moments where you forget your troubles because you've found someone who understands what it's like to live on the water. Captain Mike was proud of his strange boat, and I admired that. He didn't care what anyone thought. He was living his own adventure. For us, that meeting was a blessing. We were cold, hungry, and tired—but God had a way of placing people in our path just when we needed them most. That day, He sent us Captain Mike—and the cement boat.

They fed us. The girl told Kelly to take off those soaked red sweatpants and hang them up in the breeze that afternoon. The sun had finally broken through, warm for the first time in days. By the time we ran into them, it was mid-afternoon—the timing couldn't have been better. They started cooking, and the smell alone was enough to lift my spirits; it was heavenly. They told us they were going to motor a few more miles down the Intracoastal to a better anchorage, and they insisted we come with them.

"Come on," they said, "you'll stay the night onboard. It's calmer down there."

I laughed. "So you're actually going to show us how this cement thing moves?"

Captain Mike grinned. "Oh, she moves. Not fast—but she moves." We climbed aboard and experienced our first (and probably only) ride on a cement boat. It was slow, steady, and oddly peaceful. We laughed, swapped stories, and traded adventures all the way to their anchorage spot.

That night, they fed us a hot meal—real food—and gave us a dry place to sleep. It felt like a miracle. We talked for hours about life, travel, boats, and higher powers. They were from Michigan, friendly and genuine, and exactly what we needed right then. To me, it was more than coincidence. It was another one of those perfectly timed encounters that kept showing up when we needed them most. Just when I started to feel sorry for myself—cold, hungry, and worn down—God would send someone. This time, it came in the form of a cement boat from Michigan.

I had started to sink into that mental fog of exhaustion and self-pity, even though Florida was just ahead. But this unexpected kindness snapped me out of it. It reminded me we weren't alone on this journey. In the morning, they made us a hearty breakfast. Eggs, toast, something hot in a mug—it tasted like pure grace. We were running out of everything, and they didn't have to share, but they did. It was a small miracle, a cement oasis in the middle of the marsh. We thanked them as best we could, climbed back into our little boat, and pushed off. The sun was warm, the wind was calm, and the outline of Florida was finally just ahead.

We were going to make it.

Amazingly beautiful islands along the Georgia coastline
that we had all to ourselves

Trying to keep a positive attitude during
this seemingly endless nasty weather pattern

Cement boats actually do float!

Being taken care of and well fed

Another one of many goodbyes
as we head toward Florida

Chapter 6 -
Welcome to the Sunshine State

After looking over some charts and getting a few pointers from Captain Mike, we plotted out our next move. He pointed out a few shortcuts—routes we could take that weren't directly along the Intracoastal but would save us time. I was all for it. Our sights were set on Fernandina, a town just over the border. That meant Florida—finally, Florida. Just hearing the name gave us new energy. For us, Florida was the goal. From the very beginning, it had been the dream destination, the line we'd pictured crossing since the start of the trip. In our minds, Florida meant sunshine, turquoise waterways, warmth, and rest. Everyone goes to Florida for fun—it's ingrained in you from childhood. So now, after all the chaos of Georgia, it felt like we were rowing toward redemption. Georgia had been beautiful, sure; the marshes, the quiet mornings, the kindness of strangers. But it had also brought us two disasters—storms, exhaustion, hunger. We came out of it like two tired phoenixes, still a little singed but somehow stronger.

The sky was overcast as we rowed south, the clouds

gray and thick. But we had more energy now—food in our stomachs and real sleep under our belts. The night on the cement boat had done wonders for our spirits. The day was steady and quiet. We knew roughly where we were going, but not exactly. That's how it was most days. You had an idea of your destination, but rowing a small boat isn't like driving a car. Two miles on the water could feel like twenty. Eventually, the landscape began to change. There were hints of what we'd been waiting for—the look of Florida. We weren't exactly sure where the border was, and there was no grand celebration, no champagne, not even a proper meal to mark the moment. Just two guys, sunburned and salt-crusted, smiling at each other because we knew we'd made it. Florida. We were officially in Florida.

Before long, we spotted a marina near Fernandina Beach. We asked a few passing boaters about places to dock, and out of the few local marinas, this one got the most positive comments. When we arrived, the owner greeted us like he'd been expecting us. "Hey guys, yeah, we heard you might be stopping by, so park your boat here," he said.

"Is it safe?" we asked.

"Safe enough." He smiled. "How long are you staying?"

"Just a day or two," we said. "We need to resupply."

He nodded and pointed up the road. "If you head down that road, it'll take you straight to the beach." So that's what we did. We grabbed a small knapsack, threw on shorts and sneakers, and started walking. The plan was simple—find a room near the beach, regroup, rest up, and take in the fact that we were finally in Florida.

Like most days, we arrived late—always pushing the daylight to its limit. The walk was long, maybe a few miles, but after so much rowing, our legs welcomed the stretch. When we reached the beach town, it felt quiet—almost like off-season. A few shops, some pine trees, the sound of the ocean nearby. We found a modest-looking hotel—not fancy, but clean, and best of all, affordable. Our money was running low, so cheap and simple sounded just right. We got a room. It wasn't luxury, but it was everything we needed—a place to breathe, to dry off, and to feel human again. Best of all, we were in Florida.

We finally got to a little hotel right on the beach. It sat near the center of town—though "town" might be a generous word for it. It wasn't big, and it definitely felt like off-season. We got a room for cheap, and it was perfect. Nothing fancy, but clean and comfortable. From our window, we could see the beach and a few surfers out there trying to catch waves that barely existed. It didn't matter to us. We were just happy to have a hot shower and a real bed. That night, we cleaned up, threw on fresh clothes, and went out to a local restaurant. We were charged up—we'd made it to Florida, and we were ready to celebrate. We must have looked like a couple of kids who'd never seen civilization before, asking a million questions to anyone who'd listen.

The guy behind the counter finally asked, "So what are you guys doing, anyway?"

"We've been rowing for two months," I said.

He blinked. "You're kidding." He wasn't buying it. But a few minutes later, curiosity must've gotten the better of him because he picked up the phone—this was before cell phones—and called someone he knew at the local newspaper. He handed me the phone and said, "This guy wants to talk to you."

I get on the line, and the reporter introduces himself. "Where are you staying?" he asks.

"The hotel down by the beach," I said.

"Okay," he replied. "I'll call you tonight around 8:30 for an interview."

That was that. No visit, no camera, no handshake—just a phone call. It was a first for us. We'd been interviewed before, but always in person. Usually the reporter would show up, ask questions, take a few pictures, and Kelly and I would play off each other, filling in the blanks for the story. But this was different.

So there we were, back in the hotel room that evening—Kelly stretched out on the bed, legs crossed, hands behind his head, grinning like a man in paradise. I paced around, half nervous, half excited. The phone rang. It was the reporter. He started firing off questions—where we'd come from, why we were doing this, what our goal was. And that's when the fun started. Because depending on the day, our "reason" for the trip changed. At the beginning, we told people it was a promotional trip for Atlantic City. But somewhere along the way, "Save the Whales" became our new cause. So now, on the phone, I'm explaining both versions, trying to sound halfway official. Kelly laughed quietly on the bed, shaking his head. I hand him the phone halfway through, and he wraps it up with his usual cool, steady voice. When we hung up, we just laughed. Another strange little twist in a trip full of them. We never saw the article, never even knew if it ran—but it didn't matter. It was our first media contact in Florida, and we had no idea it was just the beginning of something much bigger to come. That night, we slept well. We were clean, fed, and in Florida—the Sunshine State. We didn't know what waited for us down the coast, but for now, we were at peace and ready to move on.

Fernandina was the start of Florida—or at least, that's what we kept telling ourselves. Like I said before, the energy, the excitement, the idea of Florida had been building in our minds for weeks. Florida meant fun in the sun, turquoise water, and palm trees swaying in the breeze. It was the finish line, the paradise after the pain. So the next morning, I wake up, pull open the shades, and look out at the ocean.

Gray. Cold. Windy. The sky looked miserable, the water rough, the air damp and heavy. I just stood there, staring out the window, thinking, This is Florida? We had crossed the border expecting to be greeted by sunshine and steel-drum music, but instead, it felt more like March in South Jersey. The dream of Florida—the postcard version—was nowhere in sight. We were two young guys, optimistic to a fault, wearing T-shirts, shorts, and sneakers, maybe a thin hoodie between us. We didn't want to believe Florida could be cold. But it was.

What we didn't realize was that northern Florida isn't the Florida you see on postcards. Crossing that border doesn't suddenly turn the world tropical. It was still winter up here, and it felt like it. So there we were, sitting in our little hotel room, looking out at the cold, gray waves. There were a few surfers out there, bobbing on their boards, trying to find something to ride. We watched them for a while, more out of boredom than anything else. I don't even think the hotel had a TV. We just sat around flipping through local brochures and magazines from the lobby, waiting for the rain to stop. It was one of those long, pointless days. No rowing, no exploring—just trying to shake the disappointment that our grand arrival into Florida had landed us in a cold, empty beach town.

I kept telling myself, This can't be the beginning of Florida. It just can't.

Still, it was probably good that we rested. We ate, we

napped, and walked around town when the weather let up. It wasn't much, but it was a break we probably needed more than we realized. The next morning, everything changed. I woke up to sunlight streaming through the curtains. The wind had died down, and for the first time in days, it felt warm. It finally felt like Florida.

We packed up our things and started walking back to the marina. The only problem was we weren't entirely sure where the marina was. We had walked away from it without much of a plan. No phone number, no map—just the memory of a direction. So we walked and walked. It wasn't around the corner. It was miles away, down what was probably a big highway now, but back then, it was just a long stretch of road through scrub and marsh. By the time we got there, it was late morning. The marina owner saw us coming and laughed.

"I was starting to wonder where you guys went," he said.

"We didn't have your number," I said. "We would've called."

He smirked. "Sure, you would have." Then he clapped us both on the back and said, "Well, I hope you make it."

"We've made it this far," I told him. "We'll see what happens next."

It was the perfect day to push off—warm, calm, and full of promise. The kind of day that made you forget all the miserable ones. We rowed out, and the world felt alive again. The waterways were busier now—boats passing, people waving, asking who we were and what we were doing. Our mood lifted with every stroke. The weather, the people, the light—it all started to feel more like the Florida we'd been dreaming of. And after everything we'd been through in Georgia, it was exactly what we needed.

Some of the boats we passed were small, some bigger, but everyone we met had the same energy—laughing, smiling, just happy to be out on the water. Maybe that's just Florida living. Whatever it was, the people down here had a vibe that was contagious. They thought we were crazy—and maybe we were—but it was the kind of crazy they could appreciate. The kind that fit right in with Florida. After weeks of marshes and isolation, it felt good to be around people again.

The waterways were livelier, and every stop seemed to turn into a small gathering. When we'd pull over for lunch or take a short break, people would wander over, curious about the boat. The big letters on the side read *Atlantic City*, which only made people more curious. They'd scratch their heads, point, and ask questions: "Where'd you guys come from?" "You rowed all the way from there?" "How long's that take?"

After so much wilderness, it was refreshing to actually talk to people again. You could feel the difference immediately. Florida had a pulse, and it was waking us up. The energy was higher, the days were brighter, and the trip started to feel fun again. This was the Florida we'd been imagining—warm, friendly, energized.

I remember turning to Kelly and saying, "You know, we've got these fishing rods, and we never use them." That hit me. I'd always dreamed about fishing in Florida. Casting a line into turquoise water, reeling in something wild. But here we were—miles into the state—and those rods were just decoration. We didn't even have a tackle box, maybe a couple of old lures rolling around in the bottom of the boat. We weren't ready to wrestle a marlin; we could barely keep ourselves fed. Still, I'd sit there staring at those rods, thinking, "Someday."

We used to have a rubber pig that we called our mascot. We hung him from one of the rods, and he would bounce around in the breeze as we rowed. But he didn't make it past Savannah. Got shredded up in the storm. The poor guy never made it to Florida. But even without our little mascot, our spirits climbed.

We were in new waters, literally and figuratively. We'd row for an hour or two, and almost every time someone would wave, honk, or motor over to talk. Big boats would blow their horns and people would shout encouragement as they passed. At first, we thought it was just friendly Florida hospitality—but then, something else started happening. A few days went by, and somehow—without us announcing a thing—reporters began finding us.

We'd pull up to a dock, stretch our legs, and someone would say, "Hey, there are two guys rowing down the coast! Is that you?" Next thing we knew, we'd be doing an interview for another local paper. I don't know how they found us—word of mouth, I guess—but it happened over and over. I think we must've been featured in five or six different newspapers across Florida, though I couldn't tell you which towns they were from. We never saw most of the articles. We'd just do the interview, have a few laughs, and then push off, not really caring where it ended up. The reporters always asked the same questions—"Why are you doing this?" "What's your purpose?" And by that point, even we didn't have a straight answer anymore. Sometimes we'd say we were doing it for Atlantic City, sometimes for Save the Whales, sometimes just for fun. The answers changed with the tide. But no matter what we told them, they all walked away smiling. And we just kept rowing—down the coast, into the sun, into whatever waited next.

Kelly filming our triumphant entrance
into the great State of Florida

Looking for another place to spend the night

Chapter 7 -
Boppin' with Mr. Blue Sky

Another day in Florida. Each morning the rhythm seemed to build on the last—our energy going to another level, our confidence growing with every mile. It felt as if Mr. Blue Sky himself was cheering us on, clearing the clouds and steering us forward. The rain had stopped completely. The skies were wide and kind. We were moving fast, maybe faster than we'd ever gone before. Everything was syncing—the oars, the current, the music on the boom box. It was like the soundtrack of our trip found its groove. Even I had to smile at how naturally it all came together. Since Fernandina, we hadn't had a single day of bad weather. Not one. No storms. No lightning. Just the steady sun above and the calm pulse of the water below. Florida had surprised me. I always pictured it as a place of quick rain bursts and thunder rolling across flat skies, but we experienced something different—something rare. The weather, the people, the pace—it all felt like grace.

The coastline kept changing moods. One moment, we'd pass fancy developed areas with bright houses and private docks; the next, we'd drift past wild stretches of untouched land that felt like stepping back in time. There was a quiet beauty in both. We'd spot small, uninhabited islands and talk about which ones might make the best camping spots. Florida wasn't all palm trees and postcard beaches, but it was beautiful in its own way—raw, varied, alive.

At every marina we stopped in, people gathered around us. Maybe it was the name *Atlantic City* painted on the boat, or maybe it was just the story. Folks would wander over, ask where we came from, shake their heads, laugh, and wish us luck. Each conversation added a little spark to the journey. We didn't know anyone, yet somehow, we always felt welcome. There was something about Florida—its sunshine, its laughter, its easy hospitality—that made us feel like we belonged there. We were living outdoors, sun-browned and free, doing something that didn't fit into anyone's routine, and that made us part of the Florida story in our own small way.

As we tic-tacked our way down the coast, we began to set our sights on St. Augustine. Everyone we met told us it was worth a stop—full of history, walkable streets, and, of course, the Fountain of Youth. We couldn't resist joking about that.

"We'll take a dip," I told Kelly, "And come out looking totally radical."

On the way there, we talked about how in South Jersey tourists were called "Shoobies." It wasn't an insult—just a local nickname for outsiders who showed up every summer. "I guess we're the Shoobies now," I said, laughing as we rowed toward St. Augustine. "Let's go do the tourist thing for once."

Kelly laughed back, and for a moment we weren't

tired travelers—just two kids on a grand adventure, joking our way through the sunshine. The water glistened. The air was warm. The oars dipped like clockwork. Everything around us said, keep going. Florida had a way of making even strangers feel at home, and for that stretch of the journey, we were right where we were meant to be.

By now, Florida had become more than a state—it was a rhythm. Each day brought its own small goals. That's how we lived the trip, one small goal at a time. Find a marina. Rest. Eat. Keep rowing. It sounds simple, but that's what kept us moving. The weather still couldn't have been better. Every morning, we woke up to calm skies and water that felt like glass. It was the kind of stretch you dream about when you plan something like this—all the conditions finally cooperating. With every sunrise, it felt like the Lord smiled down, saying, Keep going, boys. You're right where you're supposed to be.

One afternoon stands out. We glided along when a massive boat—no, a yacht—came slowly by. Back home around Atlantic City, we saw nice boats all the time, but this was different. In Florida, these things were everywhere, big enough to have their own zip codes. This one had polished decks, waving flags, and a couple standing on the stern, motioning us over. Of course, curiosity got the best of us. They waved so enthusiastically, it felt rude not to row over to them. We joked we were like trained seals whenever someone waved us over—you never knew what kind of good surprise might come with it.

As we got closer, the man and woman smiled wide. "We can't believe it!" the woman said. "We heard about you! You're the guys from Atlantic City!"

We blinked in surprise. "You're kidding," I said.

"No, really—we read about you, and now here you are!"

They introduced themselves and, sure enough, they were from the Atlantic City area—Margate, I think. They were so tickled they had actually run into us in person. Before we knew it, they invited us aboard. "Come on, check it out! You've got to see this," the man said. We didn't need to be asked twice.

The yacht was something else—polished wood, chrome details, a cabin that looked like something out of a magazine. They showed us around like proud hosts, then sat us down in the sunshine on the back deck. Sandwiches appeared and cold drinks and laughter that filled the air. It felt good—the warmth, the kindness, the connection to home. For a moment, the journey didn't feel quite so far away.

Before we left, the lady said she wanted to make sure folks back home knew we were all right. She promised to spread the word. And sure enough, later I heard from my dad that there'd been a short article in the *Atlantic City Press*—a woman had called in to say we were doing great, that she'd seen us in Florida, and that we looked strong and happy.

When it came time to go, we said our goodbyes. The woman smiled, saying, "We wish you all the best. You boys be safe out there."

As we pushed away from the yacht, I grinned and said, "Tell Pinky we said hello!"

She laughed—she knew exactly what I meant. Pinky was still getting calls from folks back home asking where those two crazy kids in the rowboat had gone.

"Don't worry," she said. "I'll make sure he gets the word." We both laughed as the yacht faded into the distance, its white hull glinting in the Florida sun. Another kind soul, another story added to the journey. It was like that the whole way—one kind meeting after another, each one reminding us God was still writing something good into our adventure. And so we rowed on—toward the next sunrise, the next small goal, and the next unexpected smile waiting somewhere down the coast.

St. Augustine was our next target—our first true tourist stop in Florida. We'd heard enough about it to know it was supposed to be a must-see, but we didn't really know what to expect. Coming from a resort town in New Jersey, we also knew how stories about "attractions" could be stretched and hyped. But at that point, none of that mattered. The journey itself had already been more than we ever imagined. We were just having fun—rolling with each day, one small goal at a time. We figured we'd make it to St. Augustine within a couple of days after leaving our last stop, but as usual, detours had their way of finding us. That big yacht visit slowed us down, and a few other encounters filled the hours, but we didn't mind. Florida had a way of teaching us that being "off schedule" was part of the adventure.

That night, we didn't stay at a marina. Instead, we found another one of those small islands scattered all along northern Florida—little dots of land barely above the tide. They became our nightly refuges. We'd pull the boat ashore, set up the tent, and laugh about how it felt like summer camp for two guys who never grew up.

The next morning, it was back to routine—Kelly making his coffee, me packing up the stove and gear, both of us getting our minds set for the day. It didn't take long to find our rhythm again. And, of course, there was the music. Always the music. That boom box cassette player became our morning soundtrack. Kelly had his favorites, and I knew when he was really into it. He'd start tossing out little slang sayings, small bursts of joy that matched the beat. That morning, as he clicked in a tape and we started loading the boat, he grinned and said, "We're just gonna bebop down to St. Augustine, man—tourists at last!"

I laughed. "Tourists! Can you believe it? We finally get to be Shoobies for once!" It became our running joke for the day—two guys from the Jersey shore, floating toward Florida's oldest city to play tourist.

The sun was out, the water was calm, and Mr. Blue Sky seemed to be keeping watch over us once again. We rowed all day. Nothing major happened—just waves from passing boats, the occasional horn, and plenty of smiles and pointing from people who probably couldn't believe what they saw: two guys in a rowboat with *Atlantic City* on the side, halfway down Florida.

The day was uneventful in the best kind of way. Peaceful. Simple. The kind of day reminding you why you started something like this in the first place. The scenery never got old. The water shimmered like glass, bending light into streaks of blue and green. Every bend in the waterway revealed something new—a stand of palms, a quiet dock, a pelican gliding low over the waves.

Looking back now, I wish we'd taken more pictures. We were too caught up in the moment to think about capturing it. Maybe that was the beauty of it—we were living it, not documenting it. We weren't racing down a highway at seventy miles an hour. We were gliding along, seeing everything slowly, letting the whole scene unfold like a moving postcard. The water, the trees, the homes, the sky—it all deserved to be remembered. But instead of reaching for a camera, we just lived it. We were just bebopping down to St. Augustine, letting the sunshine and laughter carry us along. That, to me, was what Florida was becoming—not something to capture but something to feel.

As we rounded a point late one afternoon, the skyline of St. Augustine came into view. The first thing we saw wasn't the town itself but a giant cross rising above the water. You couldn't miss it—more than two hundred feet high, gleaming in the fading sunlight. It stood as a beacon for travelers and a monument to the Christian missionaries who first brought faith to these shores. The sight of it stopped us. It was stunning—silent, steady, and spiritual. The timing was perfect too: the sun setting behind it, the sky burning gold and orange. We were tired, but that moment filled us with energy. It felt like a welcome—a holy marker saying, You've made it this far. Rest a while. A little farther on, we spotted something else: an old Spanish fort near the inlet. Its stone walls and watchtowers looked straight out of a storybook—the kind with pirates and explorers and maps that led to hidden treasure. Seeing it from the water, with the cross still standing tall behind it, was surreal. This place was already winning us over.

We'd heard about a campground nearby, so we made our way toward where we thought it might be. That part took some trial and error. In a rowboat, being off by even half a mile feels like forever at the end of the day. You start to question your decisions. But eventually, after circling the area and comparing landmarks to what we'd heard from locals, we found it. The place had everything we needed—showers, a little store, and a patch of grass where we could stretch out. We told them we might stay one night, maybe two, depending on how things went. It felt good to have a place with some comfort—especially since we planned on doing a full day of tourist stuff. And that was exactly what we did.

The next morning, after a rare hot shower and a quick breakfast, we packed the cooler and asked a local guy for directions into town. Kelly, of course, was sporting his famous red sweatpants—I don't think he ever took those things off. The man laughed, pointed the way, and sent us off with a wave. We were closer to town than we realized. Before long, we were walking through the streets of St. Augustine, soaking it all in.

The first stop was that "castle" we'd seen from the water—Castillo de San Marcos, the old Spanish fort built centuries ago. It was incredible. Thick stone walls, lookout towers, cannons aimed at the horizon. You could almost hear the echoes of history in the breeze. Inside, it felt like stepping into another time—dungeons below, watchtowers above, and the water glimmering beyond the walls. For an hour or more, we wandered around laughing, exploring, imagining pirate attacks and secret tunnels. It was pure fun. After weeks on the water, it felt good just to walk on solid ground, to blend in with the tourists, to be ordinary again for a day. Nobody looked twice at us. We weren't the guys rowing through Florida anymore—just two friends wandering through an old city, enjoying the sunshine and the stories carved in stone. When we finally left the fort, we looked at each other and grinned. The day had just begun, and for once, we didn't have to measure distance or miles. We could just be.

After we finished exploring the fort in St. Augustine, we felt like a couple of kids who'd just been given the run of a castle. The place was alive with history—cannons lined the walls, and we even heard they sometimes fired them for demonstrations. That would've been something to see. We followed our little "cheat sheet" from the guy at the campground—a handwritten list of must-see spots around town. So we left the fort behind and wandered into St. Augustine proper.

The town was beautiful. Tree-lined streets, Spanish-style buildings, and that old-world charm that made it feel both historic and alive. We spent the afternoon doing what tourists do best—wandering, laughing, and window shopping. We didn't have money to buy much, but that didn't matter. The fun was in just being there. Everything about the town felt timeless—the narrow cobblestone streets, the shaded courtyards, the soft hum of voices and music drifting from shops. At one point, we grabbed a couple of burgers, found a bench by the water, and made a long lunch of it. Nothing fancy, just two guys eating by the bay, watching the boats go by, and soaking up a kind of peace that doesn't come often in life.

St. Augustine had become one of those small goals we'd set along the way—something we looked forward to and now could look back on with a smile. We spent nearly the whole day exploring, saving one last attraction for the end—the legendary Fountain of Youth. That became our quest for the afternoon. We asked people for directions, followed signs, and joked like we were explorers on some great expedition.

"Ponce de León would be proud," Kelly said as we set off to find it.

After a long search, we finally found what we thought was the Fountain of Youth. We stood there for a moment, looking at it—a small, unimpressive little fountain, surrounded by soda cans and a few tourists taking pictures.

That was it. The legendary Fountain of Youth. We just looked at each other and started laughing. Sometimes the legend is bigger than the thing itself. It reminded me of home, back in Margate, where they've got that giant elephant named Lucy—a hotel shaped like an elephant. It sounds incredible until you've seen it eight hundred times. Then it's just an elephant with a window in its backside. So we had our laugh, took a few pictures anyway, and headed back to the campground.

That night we built a fire, cooked up what we had, and sat talking about the road ahead. The tourist day had been great, but it wasn't really us. Our hearts were already pulling south again. Something about the journey always kept nudging us—keep going. Florida is a big state. There was still so much ahead to see, and we knew the only way to find it was to keep rowing. That became our quiet mantra: enjoy what you see, and keep moving forward.

The next morning, we packed up the tent and headed out. Before long, the waterway opened into a stretch that led close to the beach. Someone had told us there was a path that would take us right to the ocean. So we pulled in—another new stop, another unknown ahead. The road was waiting. And so were we. We were finally going to see the ocean again. From where we were, it looked like about an hour's walk to the nearest beach, so we threw a few things together and started off. We weren't even sure what beach it was, but it didn't matter. The idea of stepping onto the sand and hearing the surf again was enough to get us moving.

Sure enough, after about an hour, we made it. There were actual lifeguards on duty—tall stands, red trunks, the whole deal. For a couple of Jersey guys, that felt like familiar territory.

"Let's go talk to them," Kelly said, grinning. So we did.

Turned out a few of the lifeguards were from New Jersey too—guys who came down for the winter season to work in the Florida sun. That connection made the world feel small in the best kind of way. We ended up talking with one who said he was from Avalon or Sea Isle, NJ, somewhere right along the stretch we'd rowed past months earlier.

He looked at us curiously. "So what are you guys doing down here?"

"We're rowing from Atlantic City to Miami," I said.

He blinked. "You're kidding."

"Nope. Our boat's docked just down on the Intracoastal."

That got his attention. "Really? I row a little myself," he said. "We've got some boats here. Maybe we should race sometime."

I could see it in Kelly's eyes—that spark, the competitive grin. "Yeah," he said, "we can clear out our stuff and set something up right now if you want."

I looked at him and shook my head just slightly, doing the movie director "cut" sign that meant "don't even think about it." All I could picture was some impromptu race turning into a full-blown spectacle—bets being made, egos on the line, and us somehow limping away with broken oars or bruised pride. We'd come too far for that. Kelly caught my drift. He laughed and eased off.

"Yeah, maybe next time," he said. We all laughed about it, swapped a few stories, and before long we were back on our way.

It had been fun—a little glimpse of home, a reminder of who we were before all this. But as we walked back toward the boat, we both admitted it could have easily gotten out of hand. Florida had that effect—full of sunshine, energy, and endless distractions. It was easy to get swept up in it. Everywhere you looked, there was something new to chase: beaches, people, adventure. But for us, this trip wasn't about chasing. It was about finishing. We talked about that as we got back to the boat. We'd come too far to lose focus now. Sure, we could laugh, explore, and soak in the moments, but the goal had to stay in sight—Miami.

That night, we found another marina, tucked the boat into a slip, and watched the sunset fade across the docks. Another Florida day had come and gone—full of surprises, laughter, and small lessons about staying true to the path. We were learning that focus doesn't always mean fighting distractions. Sometimes, it's just smiling at them, saying "maybe next time," and rowing on.

Finally heading into the town of St. Augustine

Castillo de San Marcos

Chapter 8 -
Other Men's Dreams

We kept leaping down the Intracoastal, and the weather—almost miraculously—continued to stay on our side. That alone felt like a gift. Rowing in those conditions made it hard not to feel energized. The water in some areas was a shade of turquoise so vivid it almost didn't look real. Every now and then dolphins would appear along the shoreline, gliding just beneath the surface. Those were the kinds of moments you'd miss if you were flying by in a powerboat. But because we were rowing, slow and steady, we noticed everything. We were awake to the world around us. We crisscrossed the channel, making better time than either of us expected. We kept up our little camping routine—primitive, but fun. Some nights we found campgrounds or small marinas. If they didn't have showers, we'd just hose ourselves down with cold water. It was simple living, but it was Florida, and in some strange way it felt like we were becoming part of the culture. Everywhere around us people were out on the water—skiing, fishing, paddling. It was its own kind of energy.

Somewhere in the back of our minds, that challenge

from the lifeguard—the guy who doubted us—still lingered. Neither of us talked about it much, but it pushed us. We started rowing farther, almost without realizing it.

We'd say, "Let's get to that point," and then one of us would say, "Actually, let's go another ten miles."

It wasn't that we needed to prove anything to him anymore; it was more about proving it to ourselves. Looking back, it's funny how one small moment like that can get lodged in you and quietly motivate you. But even as we pushed ourselves, we didn't forget the lessons we'd learned earlier in the trip. We still worked with the tides. We still avoided rowing against currents near inlets, because that was a losing battle. There were stretches of Florida where the tides weren't strong, and you could get away with it—but we didn't push our luck. Those early mistakes had burned themselves into our memory. We kept our rhythm: rowing at night when it was cooler, trying to rest during the day when the heat made everything feel heavy. It was November by then, but Florida November still felt like summer. All we knew was south. That was the only direction that mattered.

As we moved along, the water around us seemed to become more alive. Part of it was the wildlife—herons, pelicans, all the familiar birds of the coast. But the real change came with the snowbirds—people from up north migrating to their winter homes. Boat traffic picked up. Marinas felt busier. You could literally feel the season shifting, not by temperature but by people. And with more people came more conversations. That became one of the best parts of the trip. We met strangers constantly—curious, amused, or just friendly—and for us it was always easy to talk. The journey itself was an icebreaker. People started recognizing us here and there as the Blister Brothers. The name had stuck after we did a TV interview somewhere along the line. We never even saw it air—we were too busy rowing—but apparently a few folks had. Whenever we did interviews, we wore our Blister Brothers T-shirts. It was our version of first-grade marketing. Simple, but it worked.

As we kept heading south, the snowbirds arrived in force, and everything around the waterway felt busier. The energy ramped up. And that little half-day encounter with the skeptical lifeguard continued to haunt us in a strangely motivating way. We started pushing ourselves harder—setting a goal, reaching it, and then saying, "Let's go!" It wasn't pride so much as momentum. But after a couple days of that constant push, we realized we needed to stop, restock, and take a breather. Finishing up another day, we docked at one of the many marinas along the way.

There were so many that finding one was never a problem. When we couldn't find a proper campsite, we'd just throw the anchor out and sleep in the boat or pitch our tent anywhere we could. But this marina looked newer—shiny docks, clean pilings, and a row of boats that weren't just boats. These were yachts, the kind that made you stop and stare. They were off in a more private section of the marina, separate from the local and smaller vessels. Not a ton of them, but enough to make an impression.

We eased in like we always did. If there was an office open, we'd check in. If not, we'd just quietly stay the night as long as no one objected. Sometimes one of us slept on the boat and the other stretched out on the dock—cement, wood, whatever was there. After so many cramped nights in the tent, we would gladly take turns sleeping outside the boat. And the weather was still perfect for it. This place had an outdoor shower, which felt like luxury compared to rinsing off with a cold hose. There was a little convenience store—almost like a mini 7-Eleven—where we could grab snacks or whatever small supplies we needed. The marina staff, usually a manager or night watchman at that hour, told us we were welcome to stay as long as we kept to ourselves. Normally, we weren't rowdy anyway. We always tried to live up to Weinberger's advice: Be gentlemen. Keep things under control. And we did.

When everything was squared away, we settled in for the evening. Nights on the docks were always their own kind of magic. The lights from the boats shimmered on the water, the pilings creaked softly, and the Florida air wrapped around everything with a warm ease. It reminded us that despite all the miles behind us—and all the miles still ahead—this journey was still alive, still happening, still unfolding in real time. These quiet moments, just standing there looking at the water, made the whole trip feel unreal and completely real at the same time.

That night ended the way every good camping night does—just sitting still, looking around, soaking it all in. I lay back on the dock, listening to the sounds of the marina, watching the stars, and letting the whole day unwind in my mind. Kelly was probably doing the same thing. We weren't chatting much; after rowing that hard for days, neither of us had many words left. Every few minutes one of us would point out a light or a sound—"Hey, check that out"—but mostly we just existed in the moment until sleep finally won.

The next morning I woke up to Kelly rummaging around, already craving his coffee. He had a routine, and if he didn't get coffee, the day didn't start right. I told him to hang tight and ran up to the little marina shop to see what they had. It felt like luxury to buy an actual cup of coffee instead of heating water over a tiny stove. I grabbed a few odds and ends—chips, snacks, anything to break up the monotony of stale crackers and whatever else we'd been eating for miles. Inside the shop, a man struck up a conversation. He noticed me right away—by this point, I had a rough beard, sunburned skin, and the look of someone who had definitely been living outside for weeks. The clean-cut guy I was when we started this trip was long gone. Our shirts still said "Make America Beautiful," but we were anything but tidy. We looked like two guys who had been wrestling the ocean, and the ocean was winning.

The man asked what we were doing and how big our boat was—the usual questions. He was older, maybe around fifty, but in good shape and sharp as a tack. You could tell by his questions that he wasn't just being polite—he was genuinely curious. He asked about navigation, tides, and how we planned our days. Before long, he said, "Why don't we continue this conversation on my vessel? It's right over here." I didn't say no. I grabbed the coffees and went to tell Kelly. I wasn't ditching the coffee—that would've been unthinkable.

I told him, "We're not leaving just yet. I met this guy, he's staying here a couple days, he wants to make us breakfast." So we got "dressed," which basically meant putting on a clean-ish T-shirt, and headed over.

As soon as we crossed into the far section of the marina, we realized what we were walking into. These weren't boats—they were floating palaces. Perfect hulls, perfect lines, perfect everything. Kelly and I just looked at each other and laughed. Once again, we had no idea what we were getting into. The man spotted us and waved us over. When we stepped aboard, we introduced ourselves—"This is my blister brother"—and went to shake hands, but we joked that our hands were permanently shaped like oar handles. He thought that was hysterical. Then he gave us a tour of his "boat," though calling it a boat doesn't do it justice. It was a work of art—polished mahogany everywhere, gleaming brass, and every modern electronic system you could imagine.

Kelly was fascinated by all of it. He was beginning to catch the boating bug in a serious way. He wanted to know how everything worked, where everything went, how the systems tied together. Me? I was polite, but my mind was elsewhere. I was still thinking about the miles ahead, the rhythm of rowing, the next tide, the next stretch of water. Kelly was absorbing this new world. I was still anchored in the one we'd come from.

Every day on this journey felt like, Who are we going to meet next? And that morning, as Kelly and the man kept talking, I could feel something shifting. Kelly was really taking to this whole boating world. He grew up around boats, spoke the language, understood the mechanics. Me? The biggest boat I'd ever cared about was the rowboat I sat in. So while the two of them connected like seasoned sailors, I found myself just taking it all in—still amazed we were even in Florida, still amazed this whole adventure was actually happening.

After the tour, we sat down for breakfast. The man cooked like he'd done it a thousand times for guests. Between bites, he told us about his life—business success, different homes, a couple of other boats he owned. You don't have a vessel like his without being driven. He carried himself like someone who always had a plan and always got where he intended to go.

Then, mid-conversation, he leaned forward and said, "I'm going to ask you something. You're going to think it's crazy, but it isn't." Before he even said it, something in my gut tightened. He continued, "I want to put your boat on my boat. I'm heading to the Bahamas soon—maybe in a couple days, once the last bit of work is done. I've been there many times. I'll take you both with me. You can explore the islands. If you think this is cool, wait until you see the Bahamas. The water, the coves . . . you'll never want to leave."

My jaw probably dropped. Kelly didn't hide a thing—he was all in. I could practically see the adventure unfolding in his mind. Honestly, the way the man described it . . . the crystal water, the hidden coves, the sense of stepping into a whole new world—it pulled me in too. After everything we had been through, this felt like a dream within a dream. A tempting shortcut into a bigger adventure. When he said he had the room onboard and it was "no big deal," part of me believed him. Part of me wanted to say yes right then.

Kelly and I started talking about it, and I could see the tug-of-war happening between us. He asked, "Why not? Do we really have to go to Miami?" And the man clearly agreed with him. But something inside me pushed back. I couldn't shake the feeling that saying yes meant losing something—our focus, our purpose, maybe even the integrity of the journey itself. People back home were rooting for us. We'd set a goal. And while the Bahamas sounded incredible, it wasn't what we set out to do.

I told Kelly, "Maybe after we finish. Maybe we can meet him again." It was a ridiculous thing to say—how would that ever work?—but it kept us grounded.

Honestly, it was probably the most sensible thing I

could have said in that moment, even if it sounded foolish. I don't think the man was testing us. He was genuine. He meant every word. When he said he'd be leaving in a couple of days and wanted us to come with him, he meant it. And, truthfully, it amazed me how easily we could have slid into someone else's dream and abandoned our own. I walked around his boat to clear my head. My heart wanted to go, but something deeper kept whispering, Stay on course. Stay on course. I think we made the right call. It was the harder choice, not the exciting one but the right one. After about two hours of talking and imagining possibilities, we finally told him we were pushing on.

He shook our hands, genuinely wished us well, and said, "You're on your way to some great memories. Good luck, boys." Most conversations ended that way—warm, brief, and a reminder that people believed in what we were doing. And just like that, the day had only begun.

It had been a unique morning—one of those encounters leaving your mind spinning long after it's over. When we walked back to our little rowboat, neither of us said much. We were both dumbfounded. The whole idea of throwing our boat onto that man's yacht and heading to the Bahamas was wild, almost unreal. As young guys, the thought alone could knock you right off the dock. But eventually we pulled ourselves together and pushed on. The rest of the day we buzzed with energy. The encounter felt electric—here was this powerful, successful man inviting us into his world, offering us a chapter we never asked for but secretly wanted. We rowed for miles talking about "what if." And then the jokes started—"What if he drops us off and never comes back?" or "What if we get stuck in the Bahamas with no passports?" Reality sobered it up quickly. We were dreamers, but we weren't un-woken fools.

By lunchtime, we were back to our standard cuisine: the salty, soggy Ritz-and-peanut-butter sandwiches. That cheap, little three-pack had become our go-to meal. No glamour in that. As we ate, half the day already felt gone in our heads, lost to the fantasy of the Bahamas. After lunch we rowed on. Nothing major happened the rest of the afternoon; just more boats passing by, more scenery, more southern waterway life.

Eventually we spotted something ahead—what looked like a canal, maybe a marina, maybe a construction site. It was hard to tell from where we were, but we could see docks, and docks were always a welcome sign. Docks meant we might not have to spend another night sinking into mud or battling Florida bugs. As we got closer, we began to see signs posted all over: Future Site of Palm Coast Development. Sample homes. Planned community maps. The whole deal. It was clear this place was new—still being built, still figuring itself out. And not at all what we thought when we first spotted it. But it was only around three o'clock, early enough to commit ourselves to whatever this place was. So we kept rowing in. There weren't many people around—probably because it was a weekday—but there was a building that looked like an office. We knew the routine: announce ourselves, explain who we were, and hope we didn't alarm anybody too much.

We tied up, stepped out—two scruffy guys in worn-out shorts and old T-shirts—and walked into the office. The secretary behind the desk looked stunned. Definitely not the type of walk-ins she was used to. She was expecting retirees, maybe couples in their sixties wanting brochures and guided tours of the "community of the future." Instead, in walked two sunburned, bearded, salt-crusted rowers straight out of nowhere. She tried to regain her composure and asked if she could help us. We were used to that look by now, so it didn't faze us. We explained who we were and what we were doing, and she asked a few quick questions before saying, "Hold on. Let me get somebody." Then she disappeared around the corner. Whatever was coming next, we had no idea.

The man who finally came out from the back office was clearly one of the Palm Coast executives. He was dressed sharp—pressed shirt, polished shoes, the whole deal. He tilted his head at us, extended his hand, and immediately commented, half-joking, "Wow, you guys do construction or something? Your hands feel like sandpaper."

We laughed. "Something like that," we said. After weeks on the oars, our hands no longer resembled anything human.

He asked, "So what's your deal? What is all this?" So we told him. Two guys rowing from Atlantic City to Miami. Saw your docks from the water. Thought maybe it was a marina. Didn't mean to wander into the future home of a massive Florida development. And honestly, we weren't even sure if we were allowed to stay here.

He smiled and said, "Come on, let me show you around." And just like that, we were on a personal tour of Palm Coast before Palm Coast even existed.

As we walked, he peppered us with questions but also spoke with the kind of confidence only a man selling the future can have. "This is going to be huge," he said. "This whole coastline—new homes, new businesses, a whole community. It's all coming. We're selling fast. This is the start of something big." My legs were tired. My arms were tired. The truth was, the moment he started talking, I knew we weren't rowing another stroke that day. We were committed to whatever this was.

At one point I mentioned casually, "Yeah, my dad's into real estate. He's built some tract homes back where we live."

That was all he needed. "You're kidding! You've got to call him. Tell him about Palm Coast. This is going to be one of the biggest developments in the area. Perfect timing." He grabbed onto that comment like it was gold. He reminded me of that classic scene from *The Graduate*, where the older man leans in and says, "Plastics, my boy. The future is plastics." That's exactly how this guy sounded. Palm Coast was going to change everything—and he wanted us to catch the vision.

We genuinely liked him. Once again, we found ourselves in one of those surreal scenarios that kept happening on this trip. He finally said, "Listen, we have a sample home right over there. Nobody's in it—brand new, hasn't been furnished yet. But the water works. There's a shower. You two can stay there tonight. You'll be our guests of Palm Coast." It sounded almost ridiculous when he said it: our guests of Palm Coast. But he was sincere. He even called another executive over, and soon the two of them were buzzing with excitement.

Before we knew it, we were unloading sleeping bags and gear and carrying them into this brand-new, echoing model home like we were VIPs arriving for a grand opening. They thought we were the coolest thing they'd ever seen. Inside, the house felt huge—empty walls, fresh paint, construction dust, nothing but our footsteps ricocheting through the rooms. We set our things down and thanked them, telling them how amazing it was.

Half-joking, I said, "The only thing that would make this better is if a newspaper guy showed up or something." And right then—boink—a light went on behind their eyes. Both of them perked up at the same time. I'm convinced one of them was a marketing guy because the reaction was too perfect, too coordinated. What happened next . . . Well, that was about to become its own story.

The marketing guy practically lit up. He pointed at us and said, "You know what I'm going to do? I'm calling him. This is an excellent idea. I'm getting the press here. We'll set the whole thing up!" He wasn't joking. He shook our hands, thrilled with himself, and hurried out the door. The first executive—the one who had taken us under his wing—handed us the keys, so to speak.

"Stay here tonight," he said. "Put your stuff down. Make yourselves comfortable. Not much to do, but you're out of the elements."

And honestly, that was all we needed. After weeks of living in mud, salt, sun, and humidity, a roof and running water felt like a gift from heaven. I don't think he was worried about letting two scruffy strangers sleep in their sample home. Maybe it reminded him of things he'd done when he was young—times when someone helped him along. I think people saw something sincere in us. Two kids on a crazy mission, sunbaked and river-worn, giving everything we had to reach a dream. We sat on the porch of that empty model home, on the one lawn chair they had staged out front, just laughing.

"Can you believe this?" we kept saying. "We can't make this stuff up." It was surreal. One minute you're rowing in circles eating soggy crackers, the next minute you're guests of the future of Florida.

The next morning, Kelly found the coffee maker. We

ran out to get his favorite brand. I wasn't much of a coffee guy then, but this trip was slowly converting me. We rummaged through closets and found mugs. By the second cup, we were giving ourselves a tour of the place like we were buying it. They had told us not to leave early—rare instructions for us—but we obeyed.

We watched the secretary open the office and went over. She said, "The newspaper crew will be here in about an hour and a half. Can we get you anything? They're sending food over."

We felt like royalty. Sure enough, breakfast arrived—hot, good, and not from a cooler or a crumpled bag. Then the local newspaper rolled up. We gave them the story—not exaggerated, not dramatized—just honest. We appreciated what Palm Coast had done for us, and the executives appreciated what we were doing for them. They staged the photographs perfectly. Behind us, in full view, were signs reading Palm Coast—The Future of Florida. We sat in our boat for the pictures, grinning like two guys who had somehow stumbled into a marketing campaign without knowing it. The executives kept thanking us. We kept thanking them. It turned into a mutual admiration society. One of the men even took my father's address and later mailed him a copy of the newspaper. I still remember the photo: us sitting in the rowboat, the massive Palm Coast sign behind us, two scruffy kids in a sea of big dreams. Maybe we helped them sell a few homes. Maybe they just liked the story. Either way, they gave us shelter, food, encouragement, and a memory we'd carry forever. The end of that chapter, at least.

News-Journal photo by Corinne Kearfot

NEW JERSEY LIFEGUARDS MAKING 1,200 MILE ROW BOAT ADVENTURE
Daniel Steelman, left, and Kelly O' Neill stop in Palm Coast Monday

Sitting in the dock slip at the Town of the Future

Saying goodbye to Palm Coast

Chapter 9 -
Hot Wheels, Warm Meals

We moved on from the whole Palm Coast experience still amazed at how we kept falling into these situations—no plans, no preparation, nothing coordinated. Yet somehow, things always unfolded. It felt like another day where life had just begun. We rowed with more energy than ever. Looking down the line on the map, we knew we were finally hitting the stretch where everything would start trending downhill, so we really dug in. There were days on that stretch where we'd fall into a rhythm so steady it practically hypnotized you. You'd still be rowing, but mentally you were a million miles from the boat. The only things that snapped you out of it were Kelly saying something, the tape player running out of music and needing to be flipped, or spotting something strange enough that we had to go investigate. Other than that, we were cruising—pure cruising speed. No holds barred. Everything was going our way, and we were ecstatic about it.

But while we rowed along in that haze, my mind kept drifting. I started wondering about those guys from New York—the ones with the sailboat we left back in Elizabeth

City. We hadn't seen them since. Usually, we'd run into them stuck on a sandbar or passing through the same marina. But they just disappeared, blended right into the Florida boating scene. Those were the kinds of things running through my mind as we left Palm Coast behind. We eventually made it into the Daytona Beach area. As usual, we were on the hunt for supplies, a place to recharge, and maybe—if we were lucky—some kind of shower. Salt water wasn't exactly famous for making you feel fresh, and primitive living had definitely left its mark on us.

We found a pretty nice marina—one of those places that sold boats and accessories along with the normal marina stuff. We did our usual routine: "Hey, this is what we're doing . . ." And, as usual, the guy working there—typically someone not much older than us—recognized us from somewhere, or at least acted like he did.

Without hesitation, he'd point us to some place we could tie up: "Yeah, we've got room. Outside shower is over there. You guys can get situated." So that's where we stayed.

That night, while we were settling in, I found this old trash bag stuffed way under the stern seat. I had no idea what it was—hoping it wasn't old food we forgot about. I opened it up and realized it was what was left of those giant sand dollars we found back in Georgia. Just crushed white powder now. They hadn't survived the journey. A lot of our souvenirs didn't. We laughed, dumped the remains into the water, and gave them a sort of proper burial. We made light of just about everything back then. We didn't dwell on bad luck for long. We shrugged it off and kept moving. That night passed quietly. Glassy water, moonlight, barely any movement at all. It was beautiful. I've never been the type to stay up staring at the stars thinking deep thoughts—I pretty much drifted off right away. Good weather, good breeze, not too hot. A perfect Florida night.

In the morning, we ate breakfast—Kelly had to have his coffee—and then he told me he was heading out to look for film for his dad's movie camera. At the beginning of the trip, he had actually been taking real home movies. Not phones, not digital—an actual old-school film camera that had somehow survived the entire trip so far. But we never stopped anywhere that sold the right film. I can't remember if it was 8 mm or 16 mm, but he was determined to find some. And honestly, when we finally got home and developed everything, it turned out to be a pretty good movie—primitive, but good. While he was off hunting for film, I figured I'd take advantage of the outside shower.

I grabbed my stuff, hopped in, and while I was showering, I noticed this old lawn chair—ripped, rusty, definitely past its prime. But I kept looking at it, thinking, I could use this. I imagined dragging it out to the end of the dock and just sitting there until Kelly got back. So that's exactly what I did. I finished showering, carried that old chair outside, and sat down in it. Ratty or not, it worked. The sun was up, the water looked like glass, and the day was one of those picture-perfect Florida days you can only conjure up in your mind. Sitting there, watching the giant clouds roll overhead, I finally had a moment to think about the trip. And what hit me was this: every time we needed something the most—every time we were in a bind—something always came through. Someone would show up, or some opportunity would open up. Not that we didn't have trouble. We had plenty. But when things were tightest, something always broke our way. It happened over and over again. And sitting in that rusty old chair on a perfect Florida morning, it felt like it was happening again.

I was drifting off, just relaxing in that warm Florida sunshine, when I felt footsteps coming down the dock. Kelly was back. I looked over and asked, "How'd you make out?"

He shook his head and said, "I failed. Nobody has film. You'd think someone in Florida would sell camera film!" He kept going on about it while I laughed, and we both sat there, settling into the moment.

That's when we noticed this jet skier. She came flying across the water—racing at what had to be ninety miles an hour, making these wild, sharp turns, cutting so close to the dock it sent spray right at us.

At first, we just watched, then we both realized, "Wait—that's a girl!" And she was absolutely ripping that jet ski like she owned the Atlantic. We started giving her the thumbs-up, holding up fake judge's scorecards, acting like she was in the Olympics. Tens across the board. She kept whipping that thing around, carving the water like it was nothing, clearly showing off—and honestly, she had every right to. Back then jet skis weren't brand-new, but they weren't everywhere like they are today. So seeing someone fly across glassy water, tossing wakes and cutting turns like that, was a show in itself. I'm pretty sure she was test-driving it from the marina's shop. If so, they picked the right person to attract attention because she had us completely entertained. After a few minutes she spun that jet ski on a dime—one instant she was fifty yards out, the next she shot straight toward us, full speed, then stopped dead right in front of the dock. We clapped, laughing, giving her the big thumbs-up.

"You really know how to ride that thing!" we said. "What are you doing out here?"

She grinned. "I'm thinking about buying this one. They let me test it out."

"Test it out?" we joked. "Looks like you're ready to take off from Cape Canaveral!" We watched her make a few more passes, still clapping and laughing, just soaking in another one of those moments we never planned, never expected, yet somehow always stumbled into.

We watched her out on the water a little longer. Eventually she ripped back into the dock, tied up the jet ski, and headed inside. I turned to Kelly and said, "You know what? I think I just want to hang out today. I'm not really feeling like doing much. This place is cool enough to just relax." Half-joking—half dead serious—I added, "Maybe I'll even do some fishing."

I'd been dying to actually catch something the whole trip, even though every attempt so far had been a failure. Deep down I kept thinking, you're in the fishing capital of the East Coast. You should at least catch one fish. So I said it jokingly, but I meant it. Kelly climbed into the boat to mess around with his stuff while I stayed in that broken-down lawn chair watching clouds drift across a perfect blue sky.

About twenty minutes later, the jet-ski girl walked back out of the shop. And she didn't just stroll over—she strode toward us. Cocky, confident, like the kind of athletic Florida water-sports girl you'd pick out of a magazine. Sun-bleached hair, tan, that "born on the water" look. If you had three pictures of Florida beach girls lined up, you'd point at her and say, "Yep. That one."

She came down the dock and said, "What are you guys doing? What's up?"

I said, "We were watching you—that's what we were doing."

She rolled her eyes and said, "No, really."

I pointed at our rowboat and said, "See that thing? We can make that thing go about three miles an hour. What do you think about that?" She cracked up.

Kelly hopped out of the boat and joined the conversation, and soon we were giving her the whole story—our trip, the boat, how long we'd been out, where we started. She loved it. Said it was "really impressive." She told us she was really into jet skis, water-skiing, all the water-sport stuff.

She said, "Too bad I didn't bring my dog. Usually, my dog rides with me." We thought that was wild but also exactly the kind of thing she'd say. She mentioned she'd graduated high school maybe a year or two earlier—right in our age range. We grabbed sodas and talked for what felt like an hour. Easy conversation. Laughing the whole time.

Then out of nowhere she says, "Get your stuff." Not do you want to, not are you coming. Just: "Get your stuff."

We looked at each other like, "What do you mean, get our stuff? You see our stuff? It's basically nothing."

She insisted, "Get it. I want you to meet my parents. They would love you guys. I'm telling you."

We weren't doing anything else that day anyway, so we exchanged that look—Kelly to me, me to Kelly—the same "Here we go again" look we gave every time the trip threw us into another totally unpredictable situation. We had no idea where the story was going, no idea how it would end, but we were already in it. We grabbed what little belongings we had. Told the guy at the marina we'd probably be gone for the night. He didn't care. Honestly, it still amazes me how many places we left that rowboat—with our oars, our stove, our Coleman lantern—just sitting there unguarded. Losing an oar would've ended the whole trip, especially since our spare was already gone. But nothing was ever stolen. Not once. That alone felt like a miracle. Anyway, we gathered up our things, joking around with her and matching her confident energy.

Then we asked, "So . . . how do we get there? We're not rowing."

"My car's in the parking lot," she said.

We walked over—and there it was. A fire-engine red muscle car. The exact kind of car you'd never expect a girl her age to be driving. This thing looked like it belonged in a street race.

Kelly goes, "That's really cool."

And in my head, I'm thinking, Buddy, this is REALLY cool. I hadn't been in a car for over two months, and now I'm about to hop into a rocket.

She said, "There it is," and hit the unlock.

Kelly took the back seat immediately, and I slid into the front. She turned the key and the engine practically growled at us—rumbling under the hood like it had been waiting all day for an excuse to run. The marina sat tucked inside a quiet neighborhood, so she couldn't open it up right away. But even at slow speed, I could feel the power. She was looking for the seatbelts, and I was sitting there taking everything in—smells, sounds, the feel of actual seats beneath me for the first time in forever—thinking, Yep . . . this is going to be interesting.

I'm fumbling around for the seatbelt, thinking, I'm in the death seat. I would've much rather been in the back with Kelly. She tells us, "Yeah, it's about an hour away.

Just highway driving." Highway? We pull onto the on-ramp—either A1A or I-95, probably 95—and the moment those tires hit the straightaway, she floors it. The pedal goes down, and suddenly we're bobbing and weaving through traffic like we're in a race we didn't sign up for. I'm pushing my foot into the floorboard like I have some imaginary brake, and when that doesn't work, I push both feet down. I'm sweating bullets. It felt like we were strapped into a rocket ship—and she wasn't even flinching. She was three feet off someone's bumper one second, then cutting over two lanes at ninety miles an hour the next. I was freaking out.

Kelly, meanwhile, thought it was the funniest thing he had ever seen. He had owned a Jaguar and an MG—fast cars were his thing. And I'm sure he knew exactly what kind of ride we were in for. He deliberately claimed the back seat. He wanted front-row seats to my panic attack. I'm convinced the two of them were in on the joke. She kept pushing the limits, and Kelly kept egging it on from behind me, smacking me in the back of the head laughing. At one point I honestly thought she was going to pull a two-wheel turn right off the exit ramp—and she practically did.

It was the ride of my life. I'd been in a rowboat for two months, but that car ride? I'll never forget it. Eventually we made it off the highway—alive—and pulled into a quiet Florida suburb. Nice houses. Palm trees. Calm streets. A total contrast to the high-speed insanity we'd just endured. She told us she had an older brother who was either in the military or off somewhere, so it was usually just her and her parents at home. As we walked up the driveway I wondered, If she's like this, what in the world are her parents going to be like? Turns out they were some of the sweetest people we ever met.

Her dad looked retired, a little older than I expected. Her mom too. Honestly, at first glance they looked more like grandparents, but maybe that was just the Florida sun giving everyone that warm-weather look. They welcomed us without blinking, as if their daughter brought home strangers from the marina every week. She introduced us proudly—almost built us up like we were celebrities. And suddenly we were just . . . part of the family. They showed us around the house and the yard, and told us about their lives. We always listened—partly curiosity, partly respect. After all, these people had no reason to welcome two rough-looking kids into their home, yet here they were doing exactly that.

Her name was Debbie. She handed us fresh towels and said, laughing, "At least get yourselves a good hot shower." And man, did that hit the spot. After living half-wild for weeks, that shower felt like heaven. Her mom whipped up dinner—not sure she was expecting two extra mouths, but she made it work. I remember something along the lines of sloppy joes or Hamburger Helper, and it was delicious. Sitting around their kitchen table telling them where we came from, what we'd been through, all the crazy stories—those were the moments that felt unreal. Like we were living someone else's life.

Kelly went to clean up, and I stayed in the kitchen talking with them. Debbie's mom was one of the nicest people we met on the whole trip. She showed me where we'd be sleeping—a pull-out couch in the living room—and started tugging on the mattress by herself until I stopped her and helped. Kelly came out of the shower, and the three of us just settled into the simple comfort of being inside a real home again. After weeks of docks, bugs, storms, sandbars, and strangers, here we were—hot meal, warm lights, clean towels, trophies lining the shelves from Debbie's basketball and water-sports days, and a family treating us like long-lost relatives. It was right on time; exactly when we needed it. Another unexpected rescue on a trip full of them.

And that's how the night ended—safe, fed, clean, and grateful. After a night spent talking around the kitchen table, sitting outside in their backyard, and just enjoying the comfort of real people in a real home, we finally retired to the pull-out couch. To us, that couch felt like an oasis—soft, warm, and steady. No rocking water, no mosquitos, no damp sleeping bags. Just a normal couch. It was heaven.

We woke up the next morning to a breakfast that looked like it belonged in a diner—ham, eggs, toast, the works. Deluxe, no-joke, "Are we dreaming?" type of breakfast. We thanked them over and over, trying to show how much it meant to us. Hospitality like that hits differently when you've been living primitively for weeks. But in the back of my mind, I was mentally preparing myself for the ride back to the marina. I knew I wasn't getting stuck in the front seat again.

We gathered our things, said goodbye, and when we reached the driveway, I made sure—without shame—to climb straight into the backseat. That caused a good amount of laughter, but I didn't care. I'd learned my lesson. Even in the backseat, she didn't slow down. Not one bit. Speed was part of her DNA. She liked fast things—jet skis, muscle cars, all of it—and she drove like someone born with a gas pedal under her foot. Still, it had been an unforgettable evening. She was an unforgettable person—big personality, full of confidence, full of life. The kind of person that leaves a mark.

Before we left her house, she handed me something. It was a newspaper article—an old feature about her and her dog on that jet ski. A big picture of her riding full-throttle with the dog up front. I still have that picture. I can't believe I didn't lose it somewhere along the way, but it survived the whole journey.

The day with Debbie—because that's what I call it now—was just another unexpected chapter in this long string of Florida adventures. We never knew where a day was leading us. One minute we sat on a dock watching clouds, the next we tore down I-95 in a fire-red muscle car and ate sloppy joes with a stranger's family. But really, what it showed me was this: people gravitated toward the dream. Everybody, in some way, has a spark inside them—a dream, a hope, a wild idea they've tucked away. And for reasons I still don't fully understand, our journey pulled that out of people. It unlocked something in them. It made them want to help or share or invite us in. And most of the time, what came out of them was kindness—simple, unforced kindness. That day was just another example. Another story inside the bigger story. Another reminder that our dream somehow brought out the best in people.

As we moved on after our encounter with Debbie, we couldn't help but laugh. The day before, we'd covered about fifty miles in roughly forty minutes in her rocketship car—and now it would take us two and a half days to travel the same distance by rowboat. That became one of those jokes that kept us going. We needed the humor.

The day unfolded with that familiar Florida rhythm. Calm water. Sunlight dancing off the surface. Pelicans gliding overhead. And that strange contrast you only see along the Intracoastal—one side lined with beautiful homes and manicured lawns, and the other side looking untouched, wild, like it hadn't been inhabited for centuries. That always fascinated me. It made me think how incredible it would be to live somewhere along that water. And I'm positive Kelly was taking all of that in too. I know him. I'm 100 percent sure he was thinking, One day, I want to live like this.

But as we kept rowing, I felt something different settling in. Something a little melancholic. Every time we met someone—these unbelievable people with their kindness, their stories, their hospitality—we'd stay for a night, maybe two, and then suddenly . . . we'd be gone. They became snapshots in this dream we lived. Beautiful moments that existed for a day and then drifted behind us like the wake of the boat. I wasn't sad, exactly. Just aware. Aware that something unusual was happening on this trip—this way people gravitated toward what we were doing. And then, just as quickly, we were back on the water again, small specks rowing across a giant world.

My thoughts kept drifting—my mind wandered a lot during those long stretches of rowing. Hours and hours of nothing but water and sky. And somewhere in there my mind went home. My mom reminded me that Thanksgiving was only five or six days away. I had never missed Thanksgiving with my family. Ever. It was always a tradition. And now here I was, rowing in the middle of Florida. All of that—the people we met, the kindness they showed, the homes they invited us into—it made me wonder how I could ever repay it. "Thank you" didn't feel like enough. But that was all we had to offer. We didn't have much else. Just gratitude. And maybe that had to be enough.

We kept rowing south and eventually made our way to what I believe was the Titusville area. Now we were getting deep into Florida—not quite central, not quite south—just that stretch where you start realizing you've really made progress. I remember looking at the maps and realizing we were way ahead of schedule. I had expected to reach Miami near the end of December, but from what we could tell, we were easily two or three weeks ahead. That night we pulled onto the shoreline near Titusville and set up camp. The sky was clear. The air was warm. And we found ourselves saying, "Tomorrow is Thanksgiving." Who would've ever guessed we'd be right there—right then—after everything we had gone through? That was the thought that carried us to sleep. Tomorrow was Thanksgiving. And somehow, incredibly, we had made it this far. We woke up the next morning not really sure what we were going to do. Thanksgiving on the side of the Intracoastal wasn't something we had ever planned or even imagined. But like everything else on this trip, we'd figure it out.

We rowed until about noon, maybe one o'clock, before pulling into a public dock. I'm pretty sure this was one of the few spots where we actually had to pay a fee—nothing major, but it surprised me that anyone was even working on Thanksgiving Day. But sure enough, there were a few people around.

We asked them the big question: "Is there anywhere to get a meal today? Any restaurant open for Thanksgiving?"

One guy said a few places might be open, but then he paused and said, "I don't know what you'll think about this idea, but there's a local church that always does a Thanksgiving dinner for people in need. It starts around four. They've been doing it for years. It's a community thing—pretty well known." Kelly and I looked at each other.

"In need?" We were in shorts, sunburned, hauling around a rowboat full of camping gear, eating peanut butter for days on end. Yeah—we qualified. We asked where it was, and they gave us loose directions—about a half-hour walk. Nothing we weren't used to. So off we went.

Some of the walkways took us around canals, and as we walked, we saw dolphins feeding in what looked like a Thanksgiving feeding frenzy of their own—bait fish flying out of the water, dolphins slapping the surface with their tails. I was thrilled—never saw anything like it.

I'm yelling to Kelly, "Look at this! Check this out!" I'm down near the canal watching the spectacle, and Kelly's up under a tree behind me . . . when suddenly I hear him yell. I turn around and see him doing this wild dance—smacking himself, flailing, running in circles. At first, I had no idea what was happening. Turns out he was standing on a red ant nest. And the red ants were having their Thanksgiving feast—on his legs. He got swarmed. Mauled. I shouldn't have laughed . . . but I absolutely did. Couldn't help it. The sight of him running down the street, slapping his legs, yelling—it was straight out of a comedy movie. He was in bad shape though, bites everywhere.

We pushed on, him limping and complaining the whole way, until we finally reached the church. The doors were closed, but we knocked anyway. "We heard there's a dinner here for people in need," we said. They told us they had just closed the doors—but when they heard how far we'd come, they opened up and welcomed us right in.

Inside was a large hall, absolutely packed. It was the

homeless, the struggling, the forgotten of the community. And there we were—two sunburned kids in shorts and sneakers, a thousand miles from home, sitting at a Thanksgiving table with them. Kelly was in agony from the ant bites, but the guys around us—these homeless men—jumped right in with advice. Every one of them had a home remedy for fire ants. I was laughing so hard I was spitting mashed potatoes.

The way they described their solutions, with their rough humor and storytelling—it was priceless. And somehow, despite everything, it became one of the greatest Thanksgiving meals of my life. The food was good, the laughter was real, and the kindness was genuine. These men—who had so little—were doing everything they could to help Kelly in his "time of need." We were the needy ones that day. And we were fed—body and soul.

After dinner they sang some songs. The whole room lifted with this raw, unexpected joy. When we walked out, we felt like we were floating. Kelly wasn't floating physically—he was still suffering his fire-ant Thanksgiving—but emotionally we were both on cloud nine.

As we walked back I said, "I don't care where we sleep tonight. I'm good. I'm satisfied." And I meant it. It was joyful. It was humbling. It was Thanksgiving in its purest form. We were thankful—not for comfort, not for ease—but for the goodness of people God kept placing along our path.

Thanksgiving Day—taking time to regroup again

Chapter 10 - Leftovers

It was another morning—this time the day after Thanksgiving. I don't think either of us actually slept in the boat. We ended up stretched out on the dock, which probably wasn't something the marina owners would've loved, but we always woke up before anybody else ever came around. That morning, though, there was more activity than usual. Maybe it was because it was the holiday weekend. People seemed to be milling around earlier than normal. We hadn't slept late; honestly, you can't sleep late in a situation like that. Your body just won't let you.

I rolled over, started pulling myself out of my sleeping bag, and glanced over at Kelly. He looked irritated—like he hadn't slept at all. And most likely, he probably hadn't. He was still reeling from his run-in with one of Florida's natural plagues. Those things had been firing at his legs all night. As we climbed out of our bags, I could see his ankles and shins. It looked bad. Not dangerous—just miserable. It wasn't a great look, and it definitely wasn't a great way to wake up. He had that "don't talk to me yet" expression on his face, so I figured some breakfast and a new day might soften the mood a little.

I mentally went through our supplies. We definitely needed to restock before moving on. We knew there were some places nearby—more than a 7-Eleven. There was a small grocery store, not huge but big enough to get what we needed to keep the mission rolling. I figured I should handle that run and make sure we had enough to last the next day or two. After we found coffee—and something sweet, Kelly and I both did sweets so donuts were fair game—we got breakfast in us.

I laid out my plan, and he said, "Yeah, I'll hang here and try to get things ship-shaped and ready to move." That worked for me.

I started walking. And as I did, something stirred in me. I just needed to tell someone about our Thanksgiving. I don't know why. I felt this strange combination of calm and gratitude—something I couldn't fully explain. Yesterday had been . . . different. Special. There were no distractions. Normally, I'd be at the Atlantic City vs. Holy Spirit football game with my dad, who had played for Atlantic City. That was tradition. But yesterday had none of that, and yet it had more. Something deeper. That thought was still lingering as I walked toward the store. Maybe it was good I was alone; it gave me space to think.

I reached the place, and right next to the entrance was a phone booth. The moment I saw it, something in me clicked. I'm going to call my parents. That wasn't something I usually did. I'd call maybe once a week if it worked out, but calling out of the blue—especially the morning after Thanksgiving—that just wasn't typical for me. But this time I felt like I had to. So I stepped into the phone booth, dropped some coins in, and dialed home.

My mother picked up. Being the Italian mother she is, her very first reaction was panic. "What's wrong? Something's wrong. Why are you calling?" I'm standing there trying to get words out, but with her tone you'd think I was calling from the emergency room.

I said, "No, no . . . nothing's wrong. I just wanted to tell you we had Thanksgiving dinner and—" But I couldn't even get the story straight because she kept circling back to, Why are you calling? What happened? It actually started getting funny. The very phone call I wanted to make to share this peaceful, meaningful Thanksgiving memory turned into me trying to convince my mother I wasn't in danger.

My brother was there too, so I ended up talking to him for a bit. I told him about the "firing squad" that went after Kelly's legs, and he thought the whole thing was hysterical. He made a couple of comments, and we laughed. It felt good. When I hung up, I still wasn't entirely sure why I felt so strongly about making that call . . . but it turned out to be a funny, uplifting moment. Not what I intended, but still something that lifted my spirits. I walked into the store smiling, replaying my mom's worry and how she completely hijacked the conversation. I was laughing to myself as I grabbed what we needed—food, snacks, whatever would carry us through the next stretch.

On my walk back, I noticed the weather shifting. There was a little more wind, cooler than the day before. It felt like a north wind, which would actually be in our favor. That put some hope in me—maybe this was our chance to really get moving again. I came back through the gate of the marina, and right away I saw all the typical Florida activity—kids running around, people coming and going, boats being prepped. But then I caught sight of Kelly. He was standing in the water, wearing just his shorts, hands on his hips like some kind of irritated statue. I stood there thinking, What on earth is he doing now?

I walked over and said, "What are you doing? Testing out those home remedies our Thanksgiving friends told you about?" He turned around and gave me the kind of look that said, I really don't need your commentary right now, which only made it funnier.

But he stayed in the water, gritting through the discomfort, and after a minute he said, "Give me a moment. I'm in pain. I'm not enjoying this, but I'm doing it."

Eventually we got everything packed up. And once again—just like it happened almost everywhere—people started gathering around us. It was the weekend, so there were more families, more kids, more boats going in and out. People would see the oars, the name on the boat, and they knew immediately this wasn't a normal thing. They'd ask questions, and we'd tell the story. Folks were kind, curious, encouraging. That day there were maybe four or five people—two families, I think—who stood with us for a bit, listening, smiling, shaking their heads in disbelief. Finally, we told them we had to get moving. As we pushed off, they all stood there together, waving as if we were some pair of brave explorers heading off into the unknown. It was sweet, unexpected, and human. And as we rowed away, we waved back until they were just tiny figures on the dock.

The whole Thanksgiving experience stayed with me—the rejections, the shut doors, the unexpected welcome, the moments of grace, the strange beauty of it all. It felt like another one of those places in time where something bigger was happening. One of those memories that you know, even in the moment, you're going to carry with you forever.

So yes—once again—we were moving on. From what we could tell, we were entering the Indian River area of Florida. We figured it might be an interesting stretch, and it absolutely was. It was endless beauty. Endless wildlife. In fact, it was probably one of the most beautiful sections we went through during the entire trip. And the wind—at least for that first day—was behind us. That changed everything. After fighting wind for so long, having it now push us south felt like a gift. It almost felt symbolic, like nature itself was saying, "Alright boys, let's go. I'm helping you today." It gave the whole stretch this sense of ease and promise.

The next three or four days became a kind of dream. Just days of raw beauty and wilderness. We'd row for hours, pull into some quiet spot, and camp for the night. Everything around us felt untouched—still, quiet, alive. We saw dolphins constantly. We even saw what we think was a manatee with a baby beside it. This was the Florida we had imagined—sunlight on the water, wildlife everywhere, peace, freedom. It felt like drifting straight into a postcard.

We had no idea that this was the calm before the storm—that something much different was waiting up ahead. But at that moment, we were blissfully unaware. We took it all in. It felt like the Huckleberry Finn portion of the trip—no crowds, no pressure, just drifting through this wild, open water. People did pass us, though. Most were in small boats or fishing vessels. They'd go by us, catch a glimpse, and suddenly whip around to get a better look. It was almost like a game of hide-and-seek on the water. You don't expect to see a lifeguard boat named *Atlantic City* out there, so when they did, you could see the curiosity spark instantly. A boat would roar past us... then slow... then make a big looping turn and come right up alongside.

"Are you the guys?"

"Yeah, that's us." Thumbs up. Cheers. Encouragement. It happened again and again. People made sure we knew that they knew who we were—and it became funny to us. Almost predictable. But always kind. Always uplifting.

By the second day—maybe the third night—we came upon a little island. I told Kelly, "We're pulling up here. We're camping. And I'm fishing. I don't care what you say—I'm fishing today."

We had seen dolphins chasing fish, water boiling with activity, wildlife everywhere. It was paradise for anyone who loved fishing, and I couldn't take it anymore. This was the moment. Kelly, who was always the better fisherman between us, agreed.

"Yeah," he said, "we're good."

And that was that—the perfect spot, the perfect stretch of the journey, and the perfect moment to drop a line in the water. We built a fire that night. I'm not sure we were even allowed to, but we set up camp anyway. It was getting dark, and everything about the place felt right—quiet, wild, peaceful.

I had bought about twenty cans of soup earlier, not really thinking ahead. Turned out every single one was chicken noodle. So there we were again: chicken noodle soup and saltines. Another night, same menu. That's when the idea of fishing started sounding even better.

Part of fishing is the anticipation—not just catching something, but wondering what might be on the other end of the line. That anticipation was half the fun for me. The only problem was... we didn't have much in the way of equipment. No tackle box or collection of lures. We basically had a little plastic bag, a few hooks, some old weights, and one bucktail jig. That was the entire arsenal. Kelly was more patient than I was when it came to fishing, but I was determined. I rigged up the bucktail, stepped into the shallow water, and began casting. And then—I hooked something.

"Got one!" I yelled. It started jumping, thrashing around, and I started imagining the best-case scenario. "I've got a tarpon, man! If this is a tarpon . . ." But of course, life doesn't hand you tarpon on your first cast with a rusty hook. I pulled it in, threw it up on the beach, and realized it wasn't a tarpon at all. It was a ladyfish. Kind of looked like a tarpon, but definitely not one.

Kelly said, "No, keep it. We're cutting this up for bait. We'll use it to catch something bigger."

I was all in. "Yeah, that's a great idea."

The only knife we had was rusted and corroded from life in the boat, but we made it work. We cut the ladyfish into bait, rigged up a line with some weights, and cast it out again. A little while later, Kelly got a hit.

"I've got something!" he said, reeling with that excited urgency every fisherman knows. This moment was special for us. It was the only time on the whole trip when we stopped long enough to do something like this.

He pulled the fish up . . . and it turned out to be a four-pound catfish. Not exactly the glamorous "wild Florida fishing" we had pictured. The thing was flopping everywhere, and I was just glad he was the one dealing with it. Saltwater catfish down there have sharp needle-like bones on their fins, and before long—sure enough—Kelly got stabbed by one. I couldn't help it; I started laughing a little.

After the fire-ant episode, here he was again, taking another hit from Florida's natural defense system. But this time it got serious fast. He howled at first; then the pain really set in. Being stabbed by a saltwater catfish isn't a joke down there—it's well-known for being intensely painful.

Within minutes, he said, "I can't even bend my finger," and when we looked, his finger was swelling badly. Suddenly it wasn't funny anymore.

We had no ice. No first-aid kit worth mentioning. No way to get to a doctor, not in the dark, not where we were. We wrapped his finger in a rag and tried to figure out what to do, but there really wasn't anything we could do. He just had to endure it. Another night of pain for my buddy. Another lesson for me—without having to pay the consequences myself. It was like Florida had marked Kelly specifically. Fire ants one day, a catfish spine the next. We went to sleep wondering how bad it might get . . . and how it was all going to turn out come morning.

That catfish incident ended our nighttime fishing real fast. I'm sure Kelly didn't sleep at all. By morning, his finger was immovable—swollen, red, and just plain bad. I looked at him and said, "Bro . . . can you even row? Are we going to be stuck here a couple days?"

It wasn't criticism—it was concern. He needed hands more than anything on this trip. But in true Kelly fashion, he just said, "I'm going to do it." He was still in a lot of pain, but he wasn't going to let it stop us. Comfortable? Not remotely. Expected? Not even close. But sometimes on a trip like this, things just happen—things that have happened to plenty of others who ventured into these waters before. Unfortunately for us, it happened right when we needed Kelly's hands in the best shape possible. And once again, we pushed off.

I knew he was hurting, but he dealt with it. He kept rowing. We agreed to just go as far as we could, stop when we needed to, and figure it out as we went. That was the rhythm of our journey anyway—adjust, adapt, endure. During those first couple hours, maybe even most of that day, Kelly was gritting his teeth. You could hear it in his breathing, see it in his posture. Still, we were moving. That alone lifted my spirits.

What made it all feel surreal was the scenery. I kept looking around, thinking, how is this place even real? The beauty was indescribable. It was as if we had been placed there deliberately—to slow down, to take it all in. The water was quiet. The wildlife was everywhere. A few boats passed now and then, and occasionally someone would pull up to chat. At one point, a guy even tossed us some ice, which felt like a gift straight from heaven given the state of Kelly's hand.

We kept camping along that stretch—night after night in these serene little pockets along the Indian River. And as amazing as it all was, we were definitely starting to get tired of chicken noodle soup for dinner. There's only so much Campbell's you can eat before your soul starts craving real food. Kelly had been down in this region before, and one day he looked around with more energy than he'd had since the catfish incident.

"This place here—this is Sebastian," he said. "This is great."

It was encouraging to see him coming out of the worst of the pain. His finger still didn't look good, but he was talking more, pointing things out, even joking again. After rowing a day and a half in severe pain, that was a good sign.

"Look," he said, "we should try to land either here or

near here. It's looking like two more good days of rowing. Then we need to get in, rest, regroup—get ourselves back in shape." And he was right. We needed a reset. And Sebastian seemed like the perfect place to do it.

Heading south, this time on a full stomach

Chapter 11 - Simple Pleasures

What was our goal? Like I said earlier, we always carried both short-term and long-term goals in our minds. It helped us push forward. Looking back, maybe we could have reached certain places faster, but the way things were falling into place—the rowing, the teamwork, the strange mix of difficulties and beauty—it felt like the trip was being shaped for us, not by us. Honestly, I'm surprised how much rowing we did manage. I thought I'd be whining the whole way, but somehow, we pulled through. We kept going, still surrounded by wildlife every day. And then, a day or so after the catfish incident, we had a moment that every game fisherman dreams about.

It was early morning. Kelly finally felt a little better, and I felt good too. We wove between the small islands when we reached a deeper stretch of water. Suddenly we saw movement. Big movement. Not dolphins—these were larger, slower, heavier rolls across the water's surface. You could feel the power of whatever was underneath.

Rowboats are funny—they're so quiet you can drift right into things without startling them. And that's exactly what happened. We rolled right into the middle of it. Kelly took one look and said, "These are tarpon."

A fisherman's dream. Giant silver tarpon—probably pushing a hundred pounds—circling and rolling all around us. We were right in the middle of the school. You could have almost reached out and touched them. I scrambled to grab something—anything—to fish with, but Kelly just laughed.

"We don't have gear for this." And he was right. Everything we owned would've looked like a toy to those fish. So we just sat there, surrounded by these massive, rolling tarpons, watching a sight that many fishermen spend entire lifetimes hoping to see. It was beautiful. And frustrating. Painfully frustrating. Kelly had caught tarpon before. I hadn't—not landed one anyway. And here they were, right in front of me. It was like the universe saying, "Here you go; Look, but don't touch." I just took in the moment. That visual memory is burned into my mind. That was probably the last time I seriously thought about trying to fish in Florida on that trip.

Eventually, we pushed on. Sebastian Inlet was within reach—maybe half a day's row away. We got close but ended up camping on a small island for the night. I half-jokingly asked Kelly if he wanted to toss out another line. I'm pretty sure he ignored the comment on purpose. But the goal was in sight now. Sebastian Inlet—famous for fishing, beaches, natural beauty, even surfing. It was one of those "golden apple" destinations in Florida. A place where ocean, wildlife, and adventure all collided. For us, it was a chance to regroup, heal up, restock, and take a breath. We woke early the next morning, excited. We rowed for about four hours and saw what we thought was the campground. It wasn't an official campground, but there was a place to land, so we pulled the boat up on the beach, anchored it, and walked up to see if we could get a site.

It happened to be a Friday, so we figured we'd probably be there through the weekend. I grabbed the knapsack with our money, knowing we'd need to pay. We met the ranger at the entrance—friendly guy. We told him our story, and he smiled but immediately said, "It's pretty crowded in here. Let me see what I can do." We knew it was full. Snowbirds were coming in, families were out, the weekend crowd was thick.

But we asked anyway, "Is there any way we could get a site close to where our boat is pulled up?"

He laughed and said, "You're asking for prime-time campsites, guys. Take it easy."

We backed off a bit—"Okay, okay." But he was a good guy. He checked around, talked to some folks, and actually managed to get us a site close to the beach. Closer than we expected. It felt like another small gift in a trip full of odd little moments of grace. And yes—the ranger really hooked us up. It was the weekend, and I don't remember exactly how much the campsite cost, but to us it felt steep. Part of me thought, "Man, maybe we should've stayed on that island for free." But we both knew better. We needed civilization. We needed rest. We needed real facilities. We had been in "water-camping survival mode" for so long that this stop—this little slice of normal life—was necessary.

For once, we arrived somewhere in the early afternoon. By then we were pros at setting up the tent. Even though the tent itself was getting worn out—rips here, weak seams there—we got it up quickly. The campsite even had wooden chairs, a real picnic table . . . luxury by our standards. We wandered around the area, taking it all in. And despite everything I'd declared after the tarpon episode—"I'm never fishing again, not once, not ever"—Sebastian Inlet started tempting me immediately.

Sebastian had everything: surfers, fishermen, boats coming and going, a jetty stretching into the water. It was known as a great spot for all of it. Also, a dangerous inlet if you weren't careful. But to young guys like us, it was basically a playground. We had a great campsite, great weather, and the whole place felt alive. For a few hours, we walked around in this strange blend of tourist mode and seasoned-traveler mode. We didn't feel like outsiders—we felt like we belonged, like we'd earned our place there after weeks of roughing it. When we finally got back to camp, I gave Kelly a sheepish look.

"So . . . what's for dinner?"

He smirked. "We got a couple cans of soup left. And peanut butter and jelly if you want it." That became our running joke. It didn't even matter anymore. Being in such a beautiful place made the food irrelevant.

Later, as the evening settled in, I got this little itch in the back of my mind—the itch that had betrayed me countless times on this trip. "I'm going to try my luck," I said.

Kelly didn't hesitate. "Nope. I'm not coming with you. I'll be here. I'm done."

Fair enough. I grabbed my one remaining lure—one single bucktail, the last survivor of our pitiful fishing kit—and walked down to the beach. I stuck to the western side and started casting. I saw splashes, movement, the signs fishermen dream about. Over and over, I cast. And then—I hooked something. I don't know what it was. Probably a jack, maybe something else. But it took off. My reel screamed. I lit up like a kid at Christmas. I was completely in the zone, fighting this thing with everything I had. Four, maybe five minutes into the fight—snap. It broke off. I just stood there . . . and laughed. This was my final Florida fishing moment, my last attempt at glory. And of course, it ended with the fish winning. It felt perfect, in a poetic sort of way.

By the time I headed back, it was dark—an hour or two had passed. I walked up to the campsite and saw Kelly sitting at the picnic table with the lantern lit . . . and two girls sitting with him. "Wow," I thought. "Look at Kelly." They were local girls, around our age, who came to the inlet often to camp and hang out on weekends. And Kelly, of course, had found the perfect topic to win their sympathy—his finger. They knew exactly what kind of injury he had because catfish spines weren't rare around there. Kelly had entered full pity-party mode, and honestly . . . he earned it.

The two girls sitting with him were exactly what you'd expect to find at Sebastian Inlet—nature girls. Outdoorsy, confident, completely at home in that environment. They were into everything—camping, fishing, surfing, boating. The whole scene. They asked about our boat, and when we said it was pulled up on the beach, they lit up.

"You guys have a boat? Really?"

"Yes," we said. "Right over there."

Their eyes got wide. "We love shrimping," one of them said.

"Shrimping?" we asked.

"Oh yeah," they said. "We take lanterns, walk out waist-deep in the water, and as the shrimp float by, we net them."

"That's it?" we asked.

"That's it," they said, laughing. "But it's actually amazing. You get tons. Except . . . we kind of stopped."

"Stopped why?" we asked.

They exchanged a look. "We started seeing shadows. Big ones. People say there are bull sharks around here at night." That explained the hesitation. "So," they said, "if you guys could take your boat out there . . . we'd love to shrimp again." That got our attention.

They walked us through the whole setup—lantern placement, timing, where the shrimp usually drift, how to scoop them. We practiced nodding like we knew exactly what we were doing. They said, "Tomorrow night we'll do it. We'll bring a cooler full of ice. Anything we catch, we'll cook for dinner. You guys won't forget it."

I looked at Kelly. Dinner, real dinner—not soup, not peanut butter and jelly. We were sold. The rest of the day, the girls showed us around. We hung out on the beach watching surfers and fishermen. I tried not to stare too much at the fishing action, but deep down I was getting excited for the shrimping adventure. That night they invited us over to their campsite for dinner—hot dogs and hamburgers. For two guys living on canned soup, it might as well have been a feast at a steakhouse. They were great company, easy to talk to, and full of stories from growing up around Sebastian Inlet.

After dinner they asked, "You guys ready for tomorrow?" We nodded. Oh, we were ready.

They explained again: "Put the lanterns on the back of the boat. Angle the light into the water. Make sure you anchor—current can move you fast out there.

"Anchor . . ." they asked.

"Yeah, we have one," we replied. Good thing they reminded us.

An hour or so after dark the next night, we pushed off with two lanterns set up behind us. I was all in. This was as close to fishing as I was going to get. Kelly seemed to forget about his finger completely. Adventure does that to you. They gave us a long-handled net and a bucket. One of us would call out sightings—"Left! Right! Here they come!"—and the other would sweep the net across the beam of light. It didn't take long. Shrimp began drifting through the glow of the lanterns, translucent and darting. Before we knew it, we were scooping them up, dropping them into the bucket, laughing like kids. That's when I started seeing shadows. Big ones. Out on the edges of the light. Not fish. Not dolphins. Just . . . shapes. Large shapes.

"Uh, Kelly . . ." I said. "There's something out there."

He saw them too. Bigger than bull sharks? Hard to tell. But nighttime on the water makes everything feel ten times larger and twenty times more ominous. Still, we kept going. We were used to the water. And we were doing well—really well.

The girls called out from shore, "How's it going?"

"Great!" we yelled back.

Two hours later, we had a bucket full of shrimp—fresh, beautiful, perfect. The girls had their cooler ready and waiting. They packed the shrimp, grinning like they already knew how good the dinner was going to be. We felt like heroes. Turns out lots of people shrimp that way, but still—the whole thing felt like a first-time triumph. And it was the first time I'd ever gone shrimping. A full-blown success—thanks to those two girls who knew the inlet better than anyone and had the whole adventure dialed in from start to finish.

This whole shrimping experience had been a genuine success. The girls packed the shrimp the right way, like they'd done it a thousand times, and they kept complimenting us. "You guys really did well for your first time," they said.

We accepted the praise, but honestly, they were the ones who set us up for success. They told us where to anchor, where the shrimp usually drifted, how to position the lanterns. They practically coached us through it. We just followed their plan.

As we sat talking, one of them said, "You know what? Instead of staying here tomorrow and doing shrimp stuff at the campground again . . . why don't you guys come back to our place? We live about thirty or forty minutes away. You can stay as our guests. We'll make dinner and end the weekend there."

Kelly and I exchanged a look. "Yeah," we said. "Yeah, that sounds great." I added, "Would you mind stopping by a grocery store on the way? We should probably restock. We're down to our last chicken noodle soup can."

Kelly rolled his eyes like, could you sound any more pathetic? But the girls laughed and said, "Sure, no problem." We went to sleep that night feeling like we'd scored another unexpected blessing. His finger was finally improving. We'd met two people who were genuinely kind and fun to be around. The whole thing had unfolded out of Kelly's misery, but it turned into one of those side adventures that shape a trip forever.

The next morning, the girls were up early—packed, ready to go. Kelly and I followed suit, and once again we did something no sane person would do: we left everything we owned at the campsite. Our tent. Our clothes. Our gear. Everything was either inside the tent or rolled up in the boat on the beach. We didn't even question it—we just went. Logic would say someone could've easily stolen every last thing we had. But somehow, on this entire trip, these leaps of faith never turned into disasters. Things just . . . worked out. We brought our cooler, because that much we knew we needed.

On the drive, the girls said, "This is a great market. You can get everything here." And suddenly the grocery run had a whole new dynamic. Instead of two clueless guys just grabbing soup and crackers, we had female guidance. They'd watch us reach for something and say: "No, no—get that instead." "Trust us, that brand's better." "You don't want to eat that all week." It was hilarious. We must've looked like two lost boys being gently herded through adulthood. But we appreciated it.

We stocked up properly—better than we ever had on our own. After an hour or so, we arrived at their place. They lived on the second floor of a nice apartment with a big porch overlooking the area. Inside was a full kitchen, comfortable living room, bedrooms—it was a real home. To two guys living in a boat and a torn-up tent, it felt like walking into a resort. The girls started cooking dinner right away. Fresh shrimp. Real sides. Actual food—warm, seasoned, homemade. And once again, we found ourselves stepping into another little pocket of grace on this wild journey.

A real shower. A clean, warm, modern shower. I don't think either of us realized how badly we needed one until we stepped into that apartment. After we cleaned up, we sat on their porch, taking in the night air, the smell of dinner cooking, the sound of laughter drifting from the kitchen. Kelly and I kept catching each other's eyes with that expression of disbelief—How does this happen? How did we land here? We weren't thinking about the fact that we'd left our entire lives back at the campground. Our clothes. Our tent. Our boat. Everything we owned. None of it crossed our minds. We were too caught up in the comfort of the moment—in the kindness of complete strangers who had taken us in like old friends.

Dinner was incredible. They cooked the shrimp we had caught together, mixed it with pasta, spices, and whatever culinary magic they knew how to work. To us, it felt like a gourmet feast. And what made it even better was that, for the first time in a long time, we had contributed something meaningful to a meal. We weren't just two travelers saying "thank you" with empty hands—we brought the centerpiece. After dinner, we all sat in the living room while they put on music—something soft, something warm. The kind of music that makes you lean back and breathe. It was natural, easy, like the kind of night you fall into without planning it. They made up two beds for us in the living room, and that's where the night ended—peacefully, quietly, beautifully. We were exhausted. And it was the best kind of exhaustion.

The next morning, we woke up ready to face a new day. And I remember lying there thinking, How in the world does this keep happening? After all the rowing, all the camping, all the close calls, all the aches and bruises . . . moments like this would just appear out of nowhere.

Kelly was enjoying it. I was grateful beyond words. They drove us back to the campsite before heading to work for the Monday grind. When we stepped out and walked toward the tent, my heart sank for a second—What if . . .? What if everything was gone? What if someone rummaged through our stuff? We got there. Nothing had been touched. The boat was untouched. Our gear was untouched. Everything was exactly as we left it. Another quiet blessing. Another unexplainable thread woven into the fabric of the journey. Standing there on that quiet morning, I realized how remarkable the whole stretch had been. We were ending a section of pure beauty—days of wilderness, nights of camping, the serenity of the Indian River, the shrimping adventure, the hospitality of two strangers. And we were just crossing into what would become the last quarter of our journey. It was the calm before the next phase—before things ahead would ramp up, change, challenge us again. Looking back, it feels like someone—or something—was preparing us. Resetting us. Restoring us. Giving us exactly what we needed at exactly the right moment. As that perfect weekend came to a close, it felt like the chapter itself turned a page. And we were ready for whatever came next.

Leaving Sebastian, we pushed off with a quiet confidence. It wasn't an excited bebop or a burst of adrenaline—it was contentment. A steady, rhythmic stroke. We knew we had a long stretch ahead before we could resupply, but our friends had thoughtfully loaded us up with exactly what we needed. Their kindness was still fresh, and it carried us into the day. These were the kinds of days where the shoreline stretches endlessly and your mind begins to wander. An hour or two in, I felt a strange tugging, like the anchor was dragging behind us. But it wasn't the boat—it was my heart.

We had just left a portion of Florida that, from the time Kelly first dreamed up this crazy idea back in New Jersey, was the Florida I had pictured: wild and beautiful, yet alive with people who welcomed us, questioned us, laughed with us, and encouraged us. The Indian River, Sebastian . . . that whole region felt like the perfect blend of nature and humanity. It was the Florida of my imagination. Leaving it behind felt like leaving the original dream itself.

At the same time, the finish line drew closer. We were within "weeks," in a manner of speaking, of accomplishing what we set out to do. And with that realization came an odd mix of anticipation and apprehension. What was ahead of us? And what would it feel like when this was actually over? The very picture that pulled me into this adventure—that ideal of Florida—was now behind us, and it had become a surprisingly emotional thing to row away from.

As we moved on, the landscape began to shift. More docks. More houses lining the water. More boat traffic. It grew noticeably busier—like someone had turned the volume back up after a brief intermission. People waved again. Boats zoomed past. Florida's pulse beat stronger. It felt like we had reentered civilization, heading closer to whatever "the end" meant for us.

My head was full—memories of what we'd just experienced, hopes for what was ahead, and the weight of the reality that we were truly closing in. Even the songs we played affected my thoughts, sending me into different moods as we rowed. At one point I mentioned it to Kelly, and he felt it too: This is really happening. This is actually within reach. And as soon as we admitted that out loud, the joking began. That was our way of diffusing intensity.

"Why stop at Miami?" We laughed. "Why not just row right through the Keys?"

"Hey, we went through the locks in the Dismal Swamp. Why not the Panama Canal next?"

We knew it was ridiculous—but dreaming out loud lightened the mood. That was our default rhythm: talk seriously for a bit, drift into dreams and jokes, circle back again. It kept the miles from feeling heavy.

Practically speaking, the landscape changed in ways that made travel harder. With so many docks and private properties, finding a place to stop for the night got tricky. We didn't want to trespass, and the areas suitable for camping became scarce. We really had to work to find safe and respectful spots.

One night we spotted a dock that looked like the snowbirds hadn't returned yet. It seemed quiet, unused—inviting in the way only a tired rower can appreciate. We tied up at the very edge and made that our home for the night, sleeping in the boat, careful not to climb up or set foot on the dock. We were always aware of boundaries and always trying to honor those boundaries wherever we stopped. It wasn't glamorous. It wasn't perfect. But it was enough. And on this journey, "enough" had become something holy. Even so, necessity was necessity. We were always filling in the blank spaces as we went, improvising our way down the Intracoastal.

The funny thing was, even as the miles stretched on, we were having a blast. People were everywhere now—boaters, retirees, families cruising by—and they almost always slowed down or turned around just to wave at us. Some held up a thumbs-up; others shouted encouragement across the water. You'd be surprised how much a stranger's nod can lift your spirit after a long, sunbaked day. Those little moments of connection mattered. They broke up the monotony and reminded us that what we were doing wasn't invisible. It felt good. It felt appreciated. But something else was happening too—the script was flipping. Earlier in the trip, we were constantly pointing out the wild beauty around us: "Look at that bird." "Check out that stretch of untouched shoreline." "Man, this is gorgeous." Now we were saying things like, "Look at that house; check this place out!" "Oh man . . . imagine retiring there."

The scenery shifted from natural beauty to human beauty—master-planned neighborhoods, immaculately groomed lawns, homes that looked like postcards, complete with boats hanging from lifts at the ends of long wooden docks. It was the kind of place people dream of spending their retirement: quiet, sunny, organized, picture-perfect. And we had time—long stretches of time—to admire every bit of it. The architecture, the colors, the landscaping, the unique personal touches people put into their waterfront homes . . . it became this whole new world to row through. It was Florida's polished side, and it impressed us more than we expected; made to order! We were used to evaluating stretches of water based on winds, tides, and rest spots. But this was different—the entire look of the world around us evolved.

The farther south we rowed, the more refined and developed everything became. It was like the journey slowly transitioned us out of wilderness and into civilization. Part of me wanted to call my dad and say, "You need to buy a place down here!" But I had already said that a dozen times along the way, so I gave him a little break from my real-estate campaigning. Still, even with all this beauty, one thing got harder: finding a place to stop. There were so many docks and private properties now that landing spots became rare. The open, quiet patches of shoreline we used to depend on disappeared. So we stayed alert, scanning the water's edge for anything—anything—that looked secluded, abandoned, or welcoming enough for two weary rowers to tuck in for the night. It became a game of strategy, intuition, and a whole lot of faith.

No hotel fees here on our own private island

My conquering hero pose

Simple accommodations for an overnight stay

Chapter 12 - Painted Ladies

By the third day after leaving Sebastian Inlet, we were deep into the rhythm again—three straight days on the water, sleeping wherever we could, usually on those tiny islands sprinkled along the Intracoastal. Most people zipped by them without a second thought, but to us they were lifelines, little patches of sand and mangroves where we could disappear for a night and reset. We felt good. We made excellent time, the weather cooperated, and we were fully aware that each stroke pushed us into more and more populated waters.

It was early afternoon when we came around a wide, open section of the waterway. Something caught my eye—shiny, gleaming, out of place. The way a cat perks up at a flashy toy, that was us. "What is that?" I said. We rowed closer.

"That's a boat," Kelly said. But as we closed the distance, we realized this was no ordinary boat. This was a yacht—and not a small one. It was massive, gleaming white, anchored proudly like it owned the entire waterway. And of course, our curiosity switched on immediately. "Nine times out of ten," we joked, "we end up getting invited aboard."

So we had to check it out. It was practically our duty. As we approached, the thing kept growing in size. It was easily the largest vessel anchored anywhere along our journey so far—luxurious, pristine, the kind of yacht you see in magazines. We were practically giddy. But the best part? The name. Painted across the stern in elegant script were the words: *Rubber Duck*. We looked at each other.

"Who names a multimillion-dollar yacht *Rubber Duck*?" That was the moment we were doomed. What we didn't realize was that we were being lured in like characters from some ancient Greek tale—an odyssey we never saw coming. Because then we noticed movement on deck. Figures. Silhouettes.

"Sirens," I almost said out loud. These weren't just people walking around. These were models—actual models—lounging and strolling across the deck in bikinis like they had stepped out of a commercial.

The whole scene felt surreal, almost scripted. Two sun-kissed sirens here, another one over there—all of them gliding around this yacht called *Rubber Duck*. We couldn't help it. We giggled like two high school kids who'd stumbled somewhere they absolutely did not belong, and yet somehow were being invited to belong anyway. We drifted closer, slowing down to a crawl, pretending to row but obviously just gawking. If awe had a speed, we idled in it. Of course we waved—enthusiastically. They did not wave back. Not even a pity wave. That stung a little. Still, the whole thing was too good to simply pass by, so we eased toward full drift mode, refusing to abandon this bizarre, once-in-a-lifetime spectacle.

And that's when he stepped out. A man—tall, unmistakably in charge—walked onto the deck. He shaded the sun with his hand and looked straight at us. Not with annoyance. Not with confusion. But with a gesture. He lifted his finger. Curled it toward himself. And motioned: Come on over. That single finger carried the authority of a Roman emperor. That was it. All the invitation we needed. We were hooked. And we were going in. That little "come here" gesture was all we needed. One finger, and our fate for the afternoon was sealed.

We pulled the oars with purpose, gliding right up alongside the yacht. The man on deck began barking instructions, and suddenly crew members appeared from everywhere. A crew. Models onboard and a crew. Lines were tossed over the rail toward us. Ladders were lowered. Everything happened quickly, efficiently, like they'd rehearsed welcoming two clueless rowers into high society. We exchanged this look—half disbelief, half pure excitement—and climbed aboard.

Standing on the deck felt like stepping onto another planet. The man who'd waved us over greeted us with a clipped smile. He didn't look nautical at all—not weathered, not tan, not "captain-like." More like he belonged behind a desk in Manhattan, not on a million-dollar yacht. He introduced himself—something like Philip Von Blah Blah Blah. I don't remember exactly; his name dissolved in the overwhelming absurdity of the moment.

"I need to know what you guys are up to," he said, as if we were the interesting ones in this situation.

Inside, I thought, Our story? Sir, have you looked around your boat? We tried our usual humor, but it fell flat. He didn't laugh; he mostly smirked, spoke politely, and kept moving. It didn't matter. We were too busy soaking in our surroundings to care. The yacht was immaculate. Everything was top-of-the-line—polished decks, gleaming rails, equipment arranged with military precision. Even the ropes looked like they'd been combed. Philip casually gestured around as he talked: "Yes, that's my crew." "I've got a top chef on board." "My full-time captain handles most of the work." It was said so nonchalantly, like he was pointing out lawn chairs on a porch. Meanwhile, Kelly and I mentally calculated how many rowboats could be purchased for the price of a single railing on this thing.

He told us he was from New York, involved in the publishing industry, and clearly successful. Wildly successful. You don't stumble onto a yacht like this by clipping coupons. While he talked, the models—all seven or eight of them—didn't even glance our way. They drifted around the deck like a living magazine spread, sunbathing, stretching, adjusting sunglasses. It added to the surreal atmosphere, almost mystical, like the whole scene was choreographed. Models in bikinis. A full crew. A multimillion-dollar yacht named *Rubber Duck*. A New York publisher giving us a casual tour. And somehow, we were in the middle of it. We were completely engulfed—drawn in, mesmerized, amazed. It felt like stepping into someone else's dream, one stranger and more extravagant than any we had imagined. And for that moment, we were part of it.

So there we were—standing on the deck of a massive yacht named *Rubber Duck*, living in a scene that felt straight out of some bizarre movie. Two guys in a battered rowboat invited aboard a floating palace. The owner didn't know us, didn't ask for credentials, didn't even seem to care who we were—and yet, somehow, we were his guests. He told us, almost casually, "Yeah, I come down here just to unwind . . . get away from the stress." Kelly and I just nodded, trying to hide our disbelief.

"Well," I said, "looks like a pretty good plan." He

didn't share much more about his life, and oddly, he didn't ask many questions about ours either.

He noticed *Atlantic City* painted on our boat; that was about it. We gave him our usual quick version of the story—the standard intro we'd perfected over hundreds of curious onlookers—and before we even finished, he declared: "You know what? You'll be my guests tonight. We'll have dinner, hang out a bit. As the day goes on, we'll get to know each other," surveying us like zoo animals who had learned a clever trick. Just like that. Kelly and I exchanged a stunned look. We had experienced some wild moments on this journey, but this was on another level. Completely out of left field. A plot twist even we couldn't have imagined.

The afternoon unfolded like something out of a fever dream. I sat in a chair on deck, and every so often one of the models would stroll by and say hello. A few were foreign, which added a fun, awkward layer to the whole thing—it's hard enough making small talk with supermodels, let alone supermodels who barely speak English. They seemed used to the owner's eccentric invitations, so nothing about this fazed them. Meanwhile, Kelly and I tried to act normal while internally screaming, "What is happening?"

The crew had tied up our rowboat neatly—better than we ever tied it ourselves. Every now and then someone from the staff would ask if we needed anything. Water? Hors d'oeuvres? A beer? It was unreal. Then they brought out hors d'oeuvres—and not the kind you see at backyard barbecues. These looked like they were straight out of *Gourmet Magazine*. Elegant sushi rolls, bite-sized creations with flavors I didn't even know existed. Kelly wasn't too eager to try the sushi, but I dove right in and immediately started laughing. "This . . . this can't be our life right now."

As evening approached, one of the models approached us and said, "Do you guys want to shower before dinner? We have everything you need."

It hit us: we had been on the water for three days. We probably smelled like three days on the water. The offer of a shower felt like being invited to heaven. The crew showed us below deck—to a bunk area, clean towels, private showers. It honestly felt like a five-star hotel floating on the ocean. Top-notch food, pristine rooms, a staff that treated us like honored guests, and all the . . . scenery . . . one could possibly take in. Of course, we said yes. The only problem? We had nothing to change into. We hadn't exactly packed outfits for dining on a luxury yacht. When we came out of the showers, refreshed and smelling human again, all we had were the same clothes we'd arrived in: Me—an old "Making America Beautiful" T-shirt. Kelly—a well-worn Blister Brothers shirt. Two ragged rowers dressed for a convenience store about to sit down for dinner on a yacht full of professional models and a millionaire New York publisher. We didn't know how the night would go . . . but we knew one thing: we were not saying no to any of it.

There we were—two ragged rowers wearing beat-up T-shirts, both of us sporting that sun-bleached, salty look. I'm sure we appeared completely out of place. But honestly, at the time, I wasn't too worried about what these people thought. After the shower, I slipped back into my damp clothes and had this strange sense wash over me. Everything felt . . . off. Not dangerous, not threatening—just odd. Like we had stepped into a world we had no business being part of. I wandered into the lounge area where everyone seemed to be gathering for dinner. Voices filled the room, laughter echoing off polished walls. Then out came the champagne—not just any champagne, but Dom Perignon, the status symbol of the era. The crew popped three bottles at once—boom, boom, boom—like a champagne cannon salute. And somehow, we were part of it.

I found myself sitting next to a model who looked like she belonged on a billboard. She didn't seem to know what to make of me, and her questions confirmed it. They were strange, shallow, almost childlike—questions that felt more like someone poking a toy to see what it does.

"How do you paddle that little boat you have?" she asked. Paddle. I almost choked on my champagne. Kelly heard it, looked over, and gave me that classic Kelly shake of the head—his silent way of saying, You've got to be kidding me. We had rowed a thousand miles, and now we were being asked if we "paddled" our way there.

Early on, I started to sense what we were to them: entertainment, curiosities. Something to laugh about later. Not in a cruel way, just in that wealthy-people-amusing-themselves way. And yet . . . every time that thought bubbled up, out came another tray of lobster. Another round of gourmet appetizers. Another slice of the absurd luxury show unfolding before us. The owner drifted in and out, not really engaging, just overseeing everything like some eccentric ringmaster.

At one point he said, "I want to show these guys something they've never experienced." I believed him—because we definitely never had. But the more he said it, the more it felt like we were part of the entertainment for the evening. Watch these two rowboat guys from Atlantic City experience luxury. Give them more food. Hand them another glass. See how they react. What they didn't know was that we weren't as naïve as they thought. We came from Atlantic City—casinos, high rollers, fancy dinners. We had friends who worked as butlers and in penthouse suites. We knew the type, so we weren't overwhelmed . . . just rolling with the moment.

As the night went on, things grew stranger. People came and went from the room. Voices rose, laughter got louder, energy increased. It was chaotic and unpredictable—like the whole night drifted upward into some decadent, strange, magical dream. Eventually I had to step outside to breathe. I walked along the deck, feeling the cool air, trying to make sense of everything. One of the deckhands was out there, leaning casually against the rail.

I asked him, "What is this? What's going on here?"

He just laughed. "You haven't seen anything yet," he said. And the way he said it—amused, knowing, almost proud—made me realize this was normal for them. This was their routine when the owner came down with his entourage. One word kept flashing through my mind: excess. Excess in everything—food, drink, money, behavior, attention, even boredom. It was over the top in every direction. And while I wasn't uncomfortable, I was stunned. This was a world I had never stepped into, and honestly, never wanted to stay in. It was mesmerizing, overwhelming, and bizarre—all at once.

I sat there staring at the empty champagne bottles scattered around, and suddenly it hit me: Now I know why this guy named the yacht Rubber Duck. It wasn't a boat. It wasn't a vessel. It wasn't even a luxury item. It was a toy. A giant, floating toy for a man who had everything, surrounded by people who treated life the same way—like a collection of amusements to rotate through. Everything about the night was play. The food, the models, the energy, the excess. Nothing felt grounded. Nothing felt real. As I watched the chaos swirl around me, I realized how different this was from every other boat owner we'd met.

Normally, when a guy invited us aboard his boat, he'd talk about it with a kind of reverence—like the boat was part of his identity. Like the man in northern Florida who wanted to take us to the Bahamas—he had a relationship with his boat. He asked us real questions: "How do you navigate?" "How do you handle the currents?" "What's your technique for long stretches?" Boat people talk boat language. Even Kelly and I felt that. *Number 10* wasn't just a vessel—it was our home. Our teammate. Our companion. We were bonded to it. But this man? He wasn't connected to his boat at all. Other people handled every rope, every meal, every corner of the deck. He wasn't a captain—just a conductor of chaos, the overseer of an extravagant show. It became clearer and clearer that this wasn't a lifestyle—it was a performance.

The night pushed on until about two or three in the morning, and I was done. Completely spent. Drained by the noise, the surreal atmosphere, and honestly, the excess. So I slipped away. I headed downstairs to the bunks, grabbed a blanket, then went back out on deck. I found a lounge chair—but it wasn't a normal lounge chair. It was probably the most comfortable piece of outdoor furniture I've ever laid on in my life. I wrapped myself in the blanket, lay back, and just breathed. The stars, the quiet hum of the night, the faint sounds from below deck—it all felt unreal. Like we had wandered into a dream that didn't belong to us. I drifted off in that strange mix of awe and disbelief, wrapped up in the lesson—whatever lesson it was—of the *Rubber Duck*.

Morning came early. Too early. The combination of lobster, champagne, and whatever else they fed us sat heavy in my stomach. I stumbled back to the bunk area, splashed some water on my face, and tried to collect myself. Standing on deck in the crisp morning air, I stared out at the horizon and thought, What in the world is ahead of us? Whatever it is . . . let's just get moving. Eventually Kelly reappeared. I don't know where he slept—not the faintest clue—but the second he stepped onto the deck, we locked eyes. No words needed.

"Let's make tracks." I'm pretty sure he felt the exact same way I did.

We hunted down one of the crew members—our host was nowhere to be found, probably still asleep—and asked if they could drop the ladders so we could get back into our rowboat. We thanked the crew sincerely. They were good people doing a unique job, and we wanted them to know we appreciated it. We also asked them to thank the owner for the experience—even though we had no interest in sticking around for round two. We climbed into *Number 10*, pushed off, and drifted away from the *Rubber Duck*, watching the yacht shrink behind us. It felt like escaping an island. A strange island. A beautiful, excessive, disorienting island. The Isle of the *Rubber Duck.* A lesson, a story, a memory neither of us would ever forget. And with that, we rowed on.

Before I jump into the next stretch of our journey, I need to pause and speak from where I am today. This morning while reading the Word, the Lord put a verse before me that sits perfectly behind everything you're about to read: "A man's heart plans his way, but the Lord directs his steps" (Proverbs 16:9). That truth stayed with me as I reflected on the next couple days of the trip. We planned our route, our pace, and our expectations—but God directed every step, every tide, every unexpected moment. You'll be able to feel that as this part unfolds. So back to the tale.

We left the scene—left the *Rubber Duck* behind—and made a quick exit. But as we pushed off, both of us realized something was off. Our minds felt foggy, like we weren't fully functioning. It was rare for us to be cloudy at the same time. Usually, only physical exhaustion did that to us: long miles under blistering sun, rowing through pain, fighting the elements until we collapsed into sleep. But this fog was different. This was self-inflicted. The excesses of the night before had left us mentally dulled and spiritually sluggish. Still, we got to work. The exit was quick, the oars were in the water, and we were off. But the cloud mist in our minds weren't the only clouds forming. The weather shifted. The day had started sunny enough, and we didn't expect anything to hinder us, but as soon as we started rowing, the sky began to gray. Despite that, the tide actually pushed us along at a pace faster than our foggy heads deserved. Kelly definitely pulled more weight than I was. I could feel it, and I'm sure he could too—but neither of us said anything. The tide did the heavy lifting, and for that I was grateful.

As we moved forward, the sky kept darkening. I found myself praying the rain would hold off because, even in my sluggish state, the effort it took just to move forward felt like enough for one day. After about an hour, my mind began to wander—as it often did when I was tired. I started thinking about how close we were getting to the end. The finish line was suddenly real. For the first time, it felt possible that we could make it to Florida before Christmas.

When we first pushed off from Atlantic City, we figured we'd still be on the water during the holidays. That was just the reality of the journey. But now, suddenly, the end didn't feel distant anymore. It felt like something we could reach—something we could almost touch. And with that thought, every emotion imaginable hit me at once: pride, disbelief, longing, homesickness, hope. We had already come so far. Farther than most people ever thought we would. Farther than maybe even we thought we would. And yet, the Lord kept directing our steps—sometimes in ways we didn't notice until much later.

Out on the water, rowing has a way of pulling you into a drifting state of mind. No music, no noise—just the rhythm of the oars and the sound of the hull cutting through the water. As we moved along in that gray morning, my thoughts kept circling the same idea: We're really going to finish this. For the first time, it felt close—tangible. The pieces were falling into place, and barring some catastrophe, it looked like we would reach Miami by the middle of December. That realization hit me harder than expected. Normally, passing scenery on the water didn't stir up much emotion, but that morning every little thing—the tint of the water, the way the sky blended with the horizon—made me think this journey is going to be over before we know it. It was a strange cocktail of feelings: excitement, disbelief, gratitude, and a quiet kind of sadness that the adventure's end was now in sight.

Meanwhile, the weather kept shifting. The sky grew grayer, and soon the rain began to spit and sprinkle. Not a downpour, but just enough to make everything slightly uncomfortable. We kept rowing through it, but I slipped into my classic complaint mode—a defense mechanism that probably made me feel a little better but never helped

Kelly. He was most likely feeling the same as I was, but he kept things to himself. I didn't.

"What is this? Why is this happening?" I muttered. "We're rowing in the rain . . . with no raincoats . . . getting colder by the minute." I could almost hear Kelly thinking, Here he goes again, but he didn't say a word. I dug into our bag and pulled out a hooded sweatshirt, trying to get some warmth back. The rain fogged up my sunglasses until I couldn't see a thing. Finally, I blurted out, loud and irritated, "Why am I even wearing sunglasses?"

That moment was so ridiculous I think I heard Kelly chuckle. Even in the misery of it, there were flashes of humor—thin ones, but there. The rain would ease, then return, never fully stopping. We pushed ahead, quiet and thoughtful, each of us trapped in our own minds, waiting out the hours. By the time we found a place to stop, it was another one of those questionable docking decisions—some random spot we probably had no business using. But the rain had scared off anyone who might care, so we tied up and tried to set up the tent.

Setting up camp while soaking wet is an experience I wouldn't wish on anyone. We fumbled with the poles, the canvas sticking, everything slick with rain. Our clothes clung to our skin, and the cold started to settle into our bones. I'm not sure we got any real sleep that night—not with the dampness, the chill, and the weight of the long day pressing on us. That's how the day ended: wet, tired, frustrated, and unsure what tomorrow would bring. But that's the nature of a journey like this—every morning had the potential to be a fresh mercy or another test. We'd find out soon enough. Even though we barely slept, I remember lying there that night—cold, damp, and exhausted—thinking about the rain.

Not the annoyance of it, not the discomfort of rowing through it, but the blessing hidden inside it. As miserable as that day felt, the truth hit me: we had been unbelievably fortunate. For thousands of miles and countless hours on the water, we could have encountered weather like this far more often. If we had, this entire journey would have taken on a completely different tone. It would have been slower, harder, maybe even dangerous. The rain changed everything—not just the rowing, but your morale, your energy, your hope. And yet, up until now, God had spared us from it. As I closed my eyes in that rocking boat, soaked clothes clinging to my skin, that thought dominated my mind. We had been protected more times than we realized. Guarded. Shielded. Granted good weather on days we desperately needed it. The gentle rocking of the boat, the soft patter of lingering drizzle, and that realization—those were the last things I remember before finally drifting into whatever restless sleep we managed to get.

The next day felt like more of the same. The sky stayed cloudy, and the rain kept coming and going in these annoying little spurts—never enough to call a storm but always enough to dampen our spirits. Still, before we pushed off, we forced ourselves to make a cup of coffee. It wasn't our finest brew—not by a long shot—but it was something warm, and it was something normal. We needed both.

We pushed off with a determination to stay positive. Mostly, that meant putting our heads down and rowing. Much of the day felt like one long stretch of silent grinding—pulling the oars, feeling the burn, pushing forward inch by inch. It reminded me of rowing support for the Around-the-Island Swim back in Atlantic City. Twenty-five miles of steady, unglamorous rowing while swimmers circled the whole island . . . just relentless motion. That's exactly how this day felt. Not fast. Not dramatic. But steady.

By the end of the day, we finally lifted our heads and tried to figure out where we were. Ahead of us was a long bulkhead jutting out into the water. There were houses lined up along one side, but on the far end was a patch of undeveloped shoreline—quiet, sheltered, and out of the wind. To us, that was all the invitation we needed. This is it. We stop here. It wasn't raining much anymore, and that little tucked-away spot looked like mercy. So once again we pitched the tent inside the boat—a chore we usually saved for the very end of the evening because, on a sixteen-foot rowboat, setting up a tent meant gymnastics. There wasn't enough space to move around or stretch, and we certainly couldn't get out and stand anywhere. But it was the best option with the weather we had. The day had been better than the one before, but still far from ideal. The lack of sleep was catching up to us, and both of us felt it. We set up the tent, settled in, tried to occupy ourselves, and did our best to prepare for morning.

When morning came, the world finally looked different. It was Saturday, and the sky looked clearer than it had in days. We had chosen a good spot—secluded enough to hide away, but calm enough to rest. We got our things together quickly, still soggy, still cold, but hopeful. We spread out shirts, trunks, and pants across the sides of the boat, hoping the sun would dry them. It wasn't the smartest drying system in the world, but it beat rowing in wet clothes. In the back of my mind, though, I was thinking, we need a laundromat—badly. It had been way too long. But for now, sunlight would have to do.

As we pushed onward, the scenery shifted from quiet

backwaters to stretches of beautiful homes and docks—gorgeous places, the kind that make you stare a little longer than you mean to. With that came more boat traffic. More people. More energy. And that's when something shifted again. People started waving at us. Boats idled nearby just long enough to shout encouragement. Families pointed at our little vessel like we were some kind of spectacle floating through their Saturday morning. It was all ramping up—just like it had in other stretches of Florida. A fresh wave of energy flowed from the people on the water straight into us. We felt it. We needed it. And even though we were still tired and worn thin from the last two days, that rising energy gave us something to row into. The journey was waking up again.

When in need we could always pitch the tent in the boat

Chapter 13 – Fifteen Minutes of Fame

The encouragement we got from people on the water that morning felt like vitamins—super vitamins. Our moods shifted almost instantly. We chatted again, joked again, rowed the way it should feel. For the first time in days, the energy came back. As we hugged the shoreline, we drifted close to the docks and boats, partly out of curiosity and partly because it was simply fun to be near people again. The homes were gorgeous—bigger and more magnificent than almost anything we'd seen. We rowed slowly, taking it all in, letting the scenery entertain us.

Up ahead, a family—two men and a woman—stood at the end of a dock. They waved us over, motioning for us to stop. When we pulled up, they said, "We actually heard about you!" Just like that, our spirits climbed even higher. They laughed, excited and fascinated by what we were doing. They told us they'd lived along the water for years and had seen plenty of strange things, but our little Atlantic City rowboat ranked in their top-ten craziest sights.

Thinking back, we unintentionally made ourselves pretty easy to spot. Even with shirts and clothes draped all over the boat trying to dry, the giant *ATLANTIC CITY* lettering on the side still showed through. We never had an official promotional campaign, but without realizing it, we were a floating billboard. People on the water would look for that name, and the moment they saw it on a tiny rowboat with two kids inside, they knew exactly who we were. We shared our story, and they loved every minute of it.

And then—as if Florida wanted to show off for our guests—our old friends appeared. Dolphins. They surfaced and splashed not far from the dock, and no matter how many times we saw them, it never lost its magic. We joked with the family, "Well, that might be our cue to get moving. We'll just follow them!" They laughed, and we climbed back into the boat.

But when we looked across the water, something else caught our attention. A burst of activity—brightly colored sails fluttering, boats moving in all directions, crowds gathered near the shoreline. "What's all that over there?" we asked.

"Oh, the yacht club," they said. "Looks like race day. They do regattas every now and then." Race day at a yacht club—just the sort of lively scene two exhausted rowers needed.

The sun finally broke through, warming our backs. We gathered our shirts and trunks—not completely dry but dry enough—and stuffed them back into the duffel bag. People around us laughed at our makeshift drying system, and we laughed right along with them.

"Let's go," we said. "We'll follow the dolphins right to the action." The dolphins, of course, were minding their own business, but we pretended they were guiding us across the water. As we approached, the colors, the noise, the life—all of it pulled us in.

We tied off at the dock and stepped out into a bustling scene. About forty people milled around—talking, congratulating two sailors who had just won the race, relaxing on the grass near the bulkhead. It was lively, warm, and good for the soul. We blended in as naturally as two salt-stained kids from Atlantic City could. We wandered up, asked what was going on, and people filled us in on the race and the winners. The crowd at the yacht club buzzed—announcements echoing across the lawn, people congratulating the winners, everyone in high spirits. It felt like a perfectly normal race day. Nothing out of the ordinary . . . at least, not yet.

A man wandered over to us. Nothing remarkable about him at first glance—just a local-looking guy, casual, friendly. He nodded toward our little boat and said, "You two the ones in that dinghy?"

We laughed. "Yeah, that's us." And just like that, we were the center of attention again.

We told him our story—how long we'd been rowing, the miles behind us, the scenes ahead of us—and you could see the intrigue growing on his face. We asked if he owned a boat. He shook his head. "No, I'm just the caretaker for this millionaire," he said. "Guy's off on vacation somewhere. I just came by to check on his sailboat." He glanced over his shoulder at the line of immaculate vessels. "Didn't even know they were having a race today, but I've seen plenty of 'em."

He introduced himself—Eldon. Older than us by a good bit, but one of those instantly approachable Florida characters who seemed to know every inlet, every dock, every secret of the waterway. Before we knew it, we stood there with a new friend, trading stories as if we had known him for years. About twenty minutes passed that way—us chatting with Eldon, watching the activity unfold around us. The yacht club had tables set up, food coming out, people gathering in clusters.

And then, from the parking lot, something unexpected rolled in. A station wagon. Not a modern news van—this was the era before that. Just a long, wood-paneled, old-school station wagon with bright TV station lettering painted across the sides. The crowd murmured.

"Oh yeah, they're here for the race!" "They're gonna interview the winners!"

Everyone was excited. Even Kelly and I thought how cool it was to be there for this local event. We figured we'd just stumbled into a perfect slice of Florida life.

The station wagon pulled up only ten or fifteen feet from where we stood. A young newswoman got out—clearly the weekend anchor—and behind her a cameraman lugged his equipment. The winners of the race, dressed in their crisp yacht club outfits, started making their way over, ready for their moment. The cameraman set up. The microphone cables clicked into place. The anticipation grew.

Finally, one of the racers asked, "So when are you going to interview us?"

The newswoman blinked and said, "Interview you? We're not here for the race."

Everyone froze. She continued, "We're looking for the two kids rowing to Miami. We heard they were headed this way. Do you know where they are?"

The entire crowd turned and looked—right at us. And just like that, the whole scene flipped upside down in a matter of seconds. The news crew wasn't there to interview the winners of the yacht race—they were there for us. The only explanation was that someone from that family we'd met earlier had tipped them off. That had to be it. We never called anyone. We never sought attention. Yet somehow the newspapers and TV stations kept finding us.

You could feel the shock ripple through the crowd. Who? What kids? Why them? Before anyone could piece it together, Eldon just pointed and said, "Here they are. Right here." And suddenly all eyes were on us.

The news crew hurried over with questions, asking if they could do the interview for their Sunday morning show—Channel 10. People around us stared, clearly trying to understand how two ragged, sunburned kids in a rowboat could possibly be more important than the formal yacht race they'd just finished.

Normally, I was the one who took the lead in these situations. Kelly preferred to stand in the background, leaning on an oar, letting me do the talking before adding his comments. But this time, as the camera rolled and the microphone came out, I thought, "You know what? Kelly can take this one."

I stepped aside with a grin, partly amused, partly wanting to let him shine, and partly sensing this was about to ruffle some feathers. Eldon nudged me. "You know this is an insult to them, right? This race—this is their big thing."

It was then that I realized what was happening. As Kelly spoke on camera, you could hear grumbling behind us. For the first time on the trip, people were upset with us. Not because of anything we did—but because our presence unintentionally stole the spotlight. We hadn't asked for the interview. We were just there. When the interview wrapped up, the crew thanked us.

Then someone from the crowd asked, frustrated, "Aren't you going to cover the race?"

"No," the newswoman said. "It took us long enough to find these guys. We don't have time to stick around."

That was the final nail. The crowd did not want to hear that. People didn't confront us directly, but the looks—the tension—were enough. Eldon quickly pulled us aside. "Listen," he said quietly, "you guys should get moving. There's a place about a mile or two down the water called The Banana Boat. It's a restaurant right on the water. Go there. I'll meet you. We can grab lunch and regroup." It was exactly the escape route we needed. We thanked him, hurried back to the boat, and pushed off.

Once we were a safe distance away, Kelly and I finally burst into laughter. The whole thing was ridiculous, uncomfortable, and unforgettable all at once. It was just another day on the journey—another unexpected twist, another stranger stepping into our story and pointing us where we needed to go next. So off we rowed—toward a restaurant called The Banana Boat and toward whatever the next chapter of this adventure would bring, waving goodbye to the yacht club. We were still laughing about the whole situation—the grumbling yacht club crowd, the news crew showing up for us, and Eldon pointing at our little dinghy like we were celebrities who had crashed the wrong party.

We were in great spirits. The sun was out, the water was calm, and we looked forward to lunch with our new friend—Eldon, the caretaker of some millionaire's property. We wanted to hear more about that. Our minds raced too, because we had just finished a television interview with one of the biggest local stations. They aired it the next morning on their Sunday program. As we rowed, I remembered a famous saying from back then: "Everyone gets their fifteen minutes of fame." And honestly, it felt like ours had just started. What we didn't know—what we couldn't have known—was that it wasn't going to be fifteen minutes. It was going to turn into about fifteen days of craziness.

From that moment until we rowed into Fort Lauderdale, it was interview after interview, newspaper after newspaper, one thing piling on top of another. We had no clue what was coming. Back then, we didn't even read half the articles written about us. We did a couple more TV spots and never saw a single one air. We were just on the move, rowing, living day to day. Luckily, my dad took the initiative to call the stations and papers and request copies of everything. Pictures, articles—anything he could get. Thank goodness he did. Without him, we'd have almost nothing to look back on.

But in that moment, all we thought about was lunch. Rowing along the Intracoastal toward The Banana Boat felt exciting—like a reward at the end of a long, strange day. We spotted the place ahead of us. It looked fairly new—sitting right on the water, the kind of spot made for boaters. A sports-bar vibe, outdoor seating, crowds, food, music—all of it buzzing with Saturday energy. It sat right on the edge of the Intracoastal like it had been waiting for us.

As we got closer, we realized it was packed. Outdoor tables were full, crowded with people watching college football, talking loudly, laughing loudly, and soaking up the Florida afternoon. Then—before we even reached the dock—people started jumping up from their seats. "It's them! The guys from Atlantic City!" About twenty people cheered, waving us in, guiding us toward the dock. It was surreal.

Eldon had picked the perfect spot—this place was alive. The mix of locals, long-time regulars, and newly arrived snowbirds created this electric, chaotic energy. And now, somehow, the two of us rowing in only poured gasoline on the fire. We tied up, stepped out of the boat, and instantly the whole place erupted. People laughing, clapping, shouting, celebrating—kids running around, grown men slapping us on the back, complete strangers treating us like long-lost heroes. We looked around for Eldon, but he was nowhere in sight. And suddenly it hit us: We had become the spark that ignited this entire place into a full-blown frenzy. The Banana Boat wasn't just crowded—it was alive, and we had unintentionally become the main attraction.

What happened next felt like a whirlwind. I remember thinking, This is nuts. We were used to the summer craziness in Margate—places like Somers Point where things got out of hand—but this was something entirely different. We had become the fuse that ignited an entire crowd into a wild, unexpected celebration. Arms went around us. Drinks were thrust into our hands.

People kept shouting: "This is on me!" "No—let me get this!" "These guys are from Atlantic City!" Before we could get our bearings, someone got the bright idea to pass around a hat. A hat. And suddenly it was being carried around the bar by a bunch of maniacs—college kids, locals, snowbirds, everyone. The place was jam-packed, shoulder to shoulder, noise shaking the rafters. Kelly and I kept getting separated in the chaos. I'd look over and see him surrounded by people, smiling awkwardly as strangers slapped him on the back. I'd get swallowed by another group two seconds later. Finally, we managed to meet up again, both of us laughing so hard we could barely talk.

"This," Kelly said, "might be the craziest thing we've seen yet." I couldn't disagree.

Eventually the hat came back to us—overflowing. Bills falling out onto the floor. I scooped them up and started counting, half in disbelief. Six hundred dollars. Just thrown into a hat by a crowd of total strangers. I stuffed it into my pocket, barely having time to process it before more chaos spilled in our direction. The whole frenzy lasted four hours—no exaggeration. We couldn't come up for air. At one point I stepped outside to get a break and just stood near the boat trying to breathe. That's when Eldon finally showed up.

"Well, what do you think of the place?" he asked with a smirk.

"Is that really the question?" I said. Then I pulled out the wad of cash from my pocket. He nearly fell over.

"So, you already ate?" he asked.

"Ate? Eldon, we're way past eating."

We went back inside together, and the madness continued. Stories, laughter, people wanting pictures, strangers congratulating us like we had already reached Miami. The noise kept climbing, the jokes kept rolling, the room seemed to spin faster and faster. We even ended up having something like dinner—if you could call it dinner. The whole afternoon was one long, nonsensical celebration. Later, I signaled to Eldon to step outside with me.

"Alvin,"—I always called him Alvin for some reason—"thanks for recommending this. But what do you think? Should we escape before this place eats us alive?"

He laughed and said, "Well, I know another place. Not as crazy as this, but it's unique—another restaurant near the water. I know the owners. You might like it."

"Why don't you go ask Kelly if he wants to come along?" I said. "If he's in, we'll go."

So Eldon went back in first. Then I followed him—walking back into another explosion of noise. It took me a minute to even find Kelly. When I finally spotted him, he was surrounded by people—hands on his shoulders, drinks being pushed at him, everyone talking at once. He looked like he'd lived there his whole life. I finally got close enough to speak.

"Hey, Eldon wants to take us to another place. You want to come?"

He didn't hesitate. "No way. I'm not leaving here."

I laughed. "Fair enough." I pulled the wad of cash out of my pocket.

"Here—make friends. Have a good time. I'll catch up with you."

He nodded. "Yeah, man. I'm good. I'm here with friends." And honestly? He was.

I stepped back outside and walked across the parking lot with Eldon and said, "He's staying; we'll meet him later."

1970's version of a news van

A day at the races at the Yacht Club

Trying to figure out our graceful exit

Chapter 14 – Changing Times

Just as I'm settling into the idea of checking out this new place, Eldon stops and says, "There's only one problem."

I turn. "What's that?" "You can't go dressed like that. You need a collared shirt and long pants. They won't let you in wearing that . . . whatever that is."

He pointed at my soaked T-shirt and rowing trunks. "You're kidding," I said.

"Nope." And oddly enough, something about the challenge energized me. "Hold on," I said. "I've got this."

I climbed back down into the boat, which was half-shadowed in the early dark. Our duffel bag was buried under the bow seat, strapped down with bungees so it wouldn't get wet. I started unhooking everything—tired, annoyed, muttering to myself. Everything I needed, naturally, was buried at the bottom. I pulled item after item out—shirts, socks, wrinkled shorts—and the more I dug, the more irritated I became. For a brief moment I thought this trip might drive me to drink. And I haven't had nearly enough beers for that. From above, I could hear Eldon laughing softly.

"Take your time," he said. "No rush." Finally, I found a shirt. A hideous shirt—yellow with blue stripes. A button-down, yes, but one of the ugliest things I'd ever seen. Then I dug deeper and found the pants—lightweight, off-colored, the ones my mother had packed "for Florida." I knew I didn't pack them myself. All I usually wore were T-shirts and shorts. Kelly, in his fashion brilliance, only ever added his red sweatpants to the mix. But the pants and the ugly shirt would work.

So, there I was, standing in the boat, undressing and changing clothes while Eldon chuckled like he watched the world's funniest stage play. I could tell he loved this whole experience—two kids from Atlantic City, one lost in a Banana Boat frenzy, the other wrangling an outfit from a duffel bag at dusk. I threw on my sneakers and said, "Alright, I'm ready."

We got into Eldon's car, and he started weaving his tale as he drove. "I'm taking you to a place called Busch's," he said. "Old Florida. History. Celebrities come through. You'll like it." As he talked, my mind wandered. I pictured some 1940s black-and-white film—Bogart in the corner, smoke swirling, piano music drifting through a dim room. When we pulled into the parking lot, a wooden sign simply said BUSCH'S. Inside, the moment we stepped in, the atmosphere hit me. It was dimly lit. Warm. Classic. White tablecloths. Candles flickering. A bar with red stools. The air felt like old Florida charm mixed with something timeless. Instantly, it transported me back to my childhood—my grandparents' hotel restaurant in Atlantic City, the Riptide Room. They had that same intimate glow, the same dim lighting, the same classic bar. I used to sit on those stools as a kid, ordering Shirley Temples and running around like I owned the place. The memory washed over me like a warm wave. But Busch's had one thing the Riptide Room didn't—a piano.

"Let's grab a drink," Eldon said, motioning toward the bar. And in that dim, nostalgic room, dressed in the ugliest Florida shirt imaginable, I followed him—ready for whatever unexpected twist was next.

We slid up to the bar at Busch's, and instantly the bartender recognized Eldon. He didn't even need to order—just nodded, and the drinks appeared. When he asked what I wanted, I honestly had no idea. Eldon ordered something for me—some kind of martini or daiquiri with a name I couldn't pronounce. I nursed it the entire time we were there.

From the bar, I could see people gathering around the piano. A man played—sharp, confident, fingers flying across the keys like he owned the place. Eldon leaned in and whispered, "That's so-and-so," some old-time actor or singer whose name I wish I remembered. Everyone else recognized him. I didn't. But I caught the vibe instantly.

The room was dim. Smoky. People with cigarettes lifted them to their lips, and each drag lit up their faces in tiny flashes of orange. It felt like I had stepped straight into a noir film scene. And I was drinking it in.

Eldon nudged me. "Let's go up by the piano."

I almost laughed. "In this outfit? I look like a kid who stole his grandfather's Florida shirt." I imagined myself in a proper seersucker suit, white shoes, maybe a fedora tilted just right. Instead, I was wearing a yellow-and-blue striped button-down and some random Florida pants my mother had packed. But I followed him anyway.

We eased up to the piano, and it was magic. The piano man rattled off old classics—'30s tunes, '40s tunes—and the whole bar sang along like it was the last night on earth. The contrast hit me hard. Just hours before, I'd been at the Banana Boat with a mob of college kids screaming like we'd won the Super Bowl. Now I was in a smoky piano bar straight out of 1940s Florida. In one day, I had seen new Florida and old Florida, and I loved every second of it.

I wasn't sure Kelly would've appreciated it the same way. Maybe that's why he stayed where he was—with his new Banana Boat fan club. Then Eldon tapped my arm. "There's Bill," he said. I remembered the name instantly—Bill Lambrakis.

Eldon seemed to know everyone. He introduced us briefly. Bill was cordial, smiling, telling me he hoped I was enjoying myself. I told him I was—probably more than he realized. After about an hour at the piano, we drifted back to the bar. I still didn't know any of the songs, but it didn't matter. I loved the whole atmosphere. It was one of those rare moments that lands on your life like a photograph you never forget.

The night wore on. Last call came. Eldon turned to me and said, "Listen, the owner is away. There's a guest house on the property. You can stay there tonight. We'll check on Kelly in the morning." I had no phone. No idea what Kelly was doing. I could only hope he'd figure something out.

We drove maybe ten or twelve minutes until we reached a gated driveway. The place was unreal—a beautifully landscaped estate with a massive house overlooking the water and a guest house off to the side. It looked like something out of a Florida novel. Old money. Old Florida. Classic and timeless.

Eldon handed me the key. "Whatever you need, it's in there," he said. Inside was a cozy little house—kitchen, bed, everything. I stood there looking around, almost laughing. How is this my life right now? Just that morning, I'd been rowing through gray skies and questionable weather. Then a yacht club interview. Then the Banana Boat madness. Then Busch's. Now a guesthouse on a millionaire's property. It was surreal. And for the first time in a long time, I didn't have to sleep in the boat or a tent. I had a bed—an actual bed. That's how the night ended. With gratitude, confusion, amazement—and a whole lot of wonder about the journey God was writing for us.

I must have drifted off reliving everything because, the next thing I knew, I opened my eyes and it was morning. Somehow, in all the craziness, I had actually recovered. My mind was charged up again, but as I sat up on the bed, I looked around and thought: Did I really live all that yesterday? Was any of that real? And then it hit me. I had no idea where Kelly was. I had no idea where I was. I barely knew the guy who brought me here—and he was gone. Maybe I was too naïve to panic, but I figured I should just get myself together.

The guest house had everything—bathroom, shower, towels, the works. With no toothbrush, I rinsed my mouth out with water and brushed my teeth with my finger. I slipped back into the same outfit from the night before—Florida's ugliest shirt and those crinkled pants—and opened the door.

The morning light hit me, and the whole property looked even more unreal. A boathouse, a long dock, manicured grounds, the water stretching out behind the house. I felt dizzy from the sheer contrast of it all.

Then I saw Eldon walking toward me, smirking. "Well," he asked, "what did you think?"

"Way beyond anything I could've imagined," I said.

He laughed. "Want to grab something to eat before we go find your buddy?"

I shook my head. "I think we'd better go straight to the Banana Boat. I need to find him."

We drove back. It was Sunday morning, around 9:30, and the place was empty—no cars, no noise, nothing. I stood there thinking: If my night ended the way it did . . . how on earth did Kelly's end? Eldon asked if I wanted breakfast while we figured things out. I didn't know what I wanted. I was worried, amused, confused—all at the same time. We walked down toward the dock.

And there he was. Kelly. Sound asleep in the bow of the boat, curled up like a pretzel, using two of our T-shirts as a pillow—one of the worst sleeping positions I'd ever seen, but given the night he'd had, I wasn't surprised. I burst out laughing. I couldn't help it. I had imagined a million possibilities for where he might have ended up. But this—this was perfect. No phones back then. No way to check in. No way to call. If he hadn't been there, I would've been worried sick all day. But there he was. No broken bones. No stitches. No missing limbs. Just Kelly being Kelly.

I nudged the boat and said, "Wake up. Time to go."

He lifted his head, squinted at me, looked at my clothes . . . and the only thing he said was: "Nice outfit."

That one comment destroyed whatever glamorous image I thought I'd built at Busch's. All night long, I had imagined myself blending into that classic crowd—until Kelly, half-conscious and hungover, reminded me exactly what I looked like: a kid in a yellow-and-blue striped shirt, wrinkled pants, and sneakers; I wasn't Bogey but more like Dennis the Menace, and that was perfect. The whole wild sequence—from the yacht club to the Banana

Boat to Busch's and the guest house—had been one of the craziest stretches of our entire trip. It marked the true beginning of our fifteen minutes of fame. We said goodbye to Eldon, thanked him for everything, took a few pictures, and that chapter of our journey came to a perfect, ridiculous, unforgettable end.

Morning reflection at the Banana Boat

Chapter 15 - Throw Me a Lifeline

So, there we were—Kelly and I—standing on the bulkhead behind the Banana Boat on a Sunday morning. Not too early, but early enough that the world still felt quiet. Eldon had already taken off, and now it was just the two of us. We were both kind of staring out at the water, wondering the same thing: "Well . . . what next?" I was still revved up from the whole Busch's Restaurant experience—the piano, the old-Florida vibe, meeting the owner, the guest house, all of it. So I decided I needed to call my parents. I just had to tell them. For some reason, I knew they would connect to that place. I don't know why, but something in me knew it would mean something to them.

I told Kelly, "I'll be right back—I'm just going to check in."

At the end of the parking lot by the street were a couple of old phone booths—the classic glass-box, metal-frame kind. So I started walking toward them. On my way, I passed the guys at the Banana Boat who were opening up for the day, hosing down garbage cans, cleaning everything up. I was still smarting a little from Kelly's comment about what I wore the night before, so I tossed a little jab his way.

I called out to him, "Hey, do you feel like taking a shower?" Pure stupid humor—just me letting Kelly know I was thinking about him. We'd showered by hose before, so it wasn't exactly foreign.

Kelly looked at me like "Buddy . . . can you not?" But it cracked me up anyway.

I stepped into the phone booth, picked up the receiver, and dialed home. Mom answered—thankfully without the infamous, "What's wrong?!" that usually greeted my long-distance calls. Instead she was thrilled: "Oh, Danny, it's so nice to hear from you!"

I jumped right into it. "Mom, I gotta tell you something. I went to this place last night—Busch's."

Immediately she perked up. "Busch's? What's that?" I told her about the piano player, the old Florida charm, the cool vibe. I said I even met the owner—"Some guy named Bill or Al Lambrakis." She cut me off.

"Who? What did you say his name was?"

"Lambrakis," I repeated. "Bill Lambrakis. He owned the place." And just like that, she connected the dots.

"Danny . . . how in the world did you end up with Bill Lambrakis?" I could almost picture her hand over the phone, telling whoever was near, "You're not going to believe this." She and her parents had known the Lambrakis family—restaurant people know restaurant people—and suddenly everything I said took on a whole new weight. It was like I had wandered directly into a chapter of her past without knowing it. She loved it. She ate it up. And I loved that she loved it. I told her about the mansion—well, guest house, but after a night like that it felt like a mansion. I told her we ended up back at the

Banana Boat by morning. I was jabbering on, still excited, still riding the emotional high of the whole bizarre night. She said, "I can't believe you actually ended up there. It sounds terrific."

Then she said the sentence that always meant one of three things growing up: My father wanted to talk. Which meant: 1) I was in trouble; 2) I needed to listen very carefully; or 3) whatever came next was going to feel like an order from central command. He got on the line, and right on cue he opened with one of his signature phrases: "Listen, old chap . . ." That phrase alone was a red-alert siren. Something was coming.

He said he'd been talking with Kelly's parents. He'd been calling newspapers—the ones we'd told him about—and keeping track of our progress. Half the time I forgot we even gave out our route. But Dad had been following it closely.

He said, "You're getting close to the end, aren't you?"

"Yeah," I said. "Probably two or three days from Fort Lauderdale."

"That's what we thought," he replied. Then he dropped the bomb. "We're coming down. We want to see you boys finish this thing."

It threw me. I mean, we'd talked about ending in Miami like it was some mystical finish line in a fairytale. But now it was real. Parents planning flights. Parents coordinating. Parents anticipating a finish line that still felt imaginary to me. He could hear the nerves in my voice.

"Don't worry about a thing," he said. "We'll take care of it on our end."

Their plan was . . . vague, at best. Kelly would call his house when we reached Fort Lauderdale; someone there would then contact wherever my parents were expected to be landing. It wasn't a plan I loved, but Dad insisted: "Don't worry about the details. They're taken care of."

When I hung up the phone, my head was swimming. A million thoughts at once. The finish line suddenly felt real. Too real. Close enough to touch. And I wasn't even sure how to break it to Kelly—so my best idea was simply to tell him he should call his parents too. Maybe between the two of us, we could piece together what our parents had arranged while we were out here rowing our way through Florida.

I stepped out of the phone booth and started walking back to Kelly crossing the empty parking lot. He still stood where I had left him, staring out at the water, probably trying to figure out our next move—even in the state he was in after the night before. No matter what had happened, our minds always drifted south. Always toward the next stretch.

I walked up to him and said, "Hey, maybe we should get something to eat. Now that the place is open, let's grab breakfast, talk about our next move, get our heads together."

"Yeah," he said, "that sounds good."

It was nothing like the chaos of the night before. No crowds. No cheering. Just two ragged guys wanting eggs and coffee. The morning crew didn't know who we were. They sat us in the front, looking out over the water. We ordered breakfast, and once the plates hit the table, I had to break the news.

"Kel, listen . . . you're gonna have to call your parents after this. Something's brewing, and I'm not totally sure what it is."

He stared at me. Or maybe through me. "Call my parents? Why? What happened?"

I tried to explain it the best I could. "Well . . . they're cooking up some kind of adventure of their own. They want to come down and watch us row into Miami. Whatever that means." Truthfully, neither of us knew what "rowing into Miami" even looked like. It was a dream we kept tossing around, but we'd never pictured the details. Still, I dumped this one in Kelly's lap because I'd been told everything was "handled on their end." And of course, this was the worst possible timing to tell him. He was still emotionally scrambled from the night before. But it was thrown in my lap, so now it was thrown in his.

Just then, someone approached the table. "You guys are the ones in that boat, right?" And just like that—boom—the spark returned. The recognition, the attention, the little vitamin shot of fifteen-minutes-of-fame energy. Kelly perked up. It was exactly what he needed—better than Florida orange juice.

We finished breakfast, and when the check came—it was maybe fifteen bucks—I said, "Alright, no problem, grab the money and let's go."

Silence. Then Kelly said, "I . . . don't have the money."

"What do you mean you don't have the money?"

"I spent it all. Buying people drinks."

I couldn't help it—I burst out laughing. Easy come, easy go. It wasn't even our money originally. When I had handed it to him the night before, I practically said, "Have a great time! Party on!" And he did—exactly that.

We dug out what we had left, covered the breakfast, and pulled out our charts. The plan was simple: follow the Intracoastal Waterway south. No tricks. No surprises. Just keep the bow pointed forward. I pointed to the phone booths.

"Alright, let's put this to bed. Call your folks." Kelly

walked toward the phone like he was heading to the gallows. Step by step by step. He didn't want to make the call, but he did. And sure enough, he was on the phone a good fifteen minutes—which for us was an eternity. While he talked, I got the boat ready.

When he finally returned, I asked, "How'd it go?"

He said, "Yeah . . . they're coming down. Two or three days. Somewhere in the area . . . I forget exactly where. We just gotta call when we know we're close." It wasn't much of a plan, but it was their plan. And somehow, we were supposed to row into it.

We shoved off later than usual. The whole morning had been a circus of phone calls, emotions, logistics, and leftover insanity from the night before. But finally—finally—we were back on the water. And man, what a beautiful day. As we pushed away from the Banana Boat, I was cracking up. So much had happened in that one little square of Florida. The chaos, the excitement, the money, the people shouting "There go the guys!" like we were celebrities drifting out of their lives. A few people waved as we rowed past. Thumbs-up. Smiles. Those tiny reminders we were part of something bigger now—a story people were following.

I felt a strange mix of emotions. Part pride. Part nerves. Part disbelief we were actually this close to the end. Inches, in my mind—but not really. We still had a good stretch left. Still miles of backwater Intracoastal to cover. But we pointed the bow south, dipped the oars, and moved forward. Off we went.

Once again, we rolled down the Intracoastal. And even after all the miles behind us, I still couldn't get over the mixture of raw beauty and nonstop development. It amazed me. One moment the water was this unreal turquoise, shimmering like something out of a travel brochure, and then—just beyond that—stood palm trees, mangroves, birds tucked into the branches, and mansions lined up like royalty watching us go by. It was endless. Like postcards strung together in a reel. People always say, "You gotta see it to believe it." And it's true—your own eyes take pictures ten times better than any camera ever could. Every bend in the water was another breathtaking snapshot burned into my memory. Even after weeks on the water, the wonder never stopped.

Rowing had become effortless by then. It was just part of being alive, part of being in that boat. Sure, we had to pay attention in tighter spots, but most of the time we flided, almost daydreaming—until someone would come flying by and holler: "Yo! You're the guys—the rowing dudes!" Every time, it snapped us out of whatever quiet trance we were in. We'd wave, thumbs up, smile. Boats big and small moved around us—sport fishermen, cruisers, yachts that looked like floating hotels. The whole scene was top-shelf: the nature, the development, the wealth, the wildlife. Everything was dialed up to the highest setting. I still say that when you race through an area in a fast boat, you miss the best parts. But rowing? Rowing lets you see everything. Every detail. You feel the place.

By late afternoon, I had finally put the madness of the morning behind me. The beauty of the day had swallowed it whole. Even though we started three or four hours later than normal, we made incredible progress—easily twenty miles. Now we were in "dockage mode," scanning for somewhere to sleep. Kelly definitely didn't want another night in the boat. But options weren't great in these highly developed areas. Still, small pockets of natural islands were tucked between all the mansions and marinas.

Kelly—our forward lookout—suddenly pointed. "Look! There's a beach." And there it was: a small sandy cutout, shaped like it had been designed just for us.

We pulled the boat up onto the beach. No one around, no one to bother us. Made to order. We dragged the boat clear, dropped the anchor, and realized—for once—we didn't have to pitch the tent inside the boat. We set the tent up on dry sand, cooked dinner on our little stove for the first time in a while, and soaked everything in. Chicken noodle soup and crackers never tasted so good. It was the perfect combination—a beautiful end to a strange couple of days and an even stranger morning.

As darkness settled in, the whole world transformed. The sky deepened, stars appeared, and across the water the mansions lit up one by one. Dock lights reflected on the turquoise water, shimmering gold and white like ornaments. It felt like we watched Florida decorate itself for Christmas. A giant holiday display stretched across the shoreline—boats, docks, boathouses, palms, all glowing in the warm lights. It wasn't natural, but it was breathtaking. And in that moment, camping under the stars while looking out at million-dollar homes, it felt like our own unique version of Christmas in Florida.

We sat there talking quietly, knowing the journey was coming to an end sooner than later. At this pace, we might actually hit Fort Lauderdale next. Kelly said, "We should be a little professional about this. My dad told me about a marina—Bahia Mar Marina. Supposed to be really nice." Another funny name in a long list of strange episodes. But he said it with confidence, and that was enough for me.

"Cool," I said. "I'm in." I half listened, half stared at the water, still absorbing everything. But I heard what mattered; tomorrow's destination: Fort Lauderdale. The Bahia Mar Marina. One of the oldest, coolest marinas on the Intracoastal. And now it was where we were headed.

Morning arrived fast. Kelly was already up. He had completely shaken off whatever was left from the previous couple of days—and honestly, so had I. We were jazzed. Something in the air felt big. We were heading into something that, in our wildest dreams, we could never have imagined, and we both knew it. We looked at each other and did our handshake—if you could even call it that. It wasn't a real handshake. We curled our fingers like claws, the way you hold an oar, and tapped hands. It was our symbol. Our way of saying we've come far. We've hurt. We've endured. And we're still together in this. Everything we'd gone through was in that handshake. It was the perfect sendoff. We pushed out into the water with a strange mix of excitement, gratitude, fear, and disbelief. Our goal—once just talk, just a fantasy we'd toss out casually in Maryland or Virginia—was suddenly close enough to touch.

Boats were everywhere. More traffic than ever. Every now and then a horn would blast, just a quick acknowledgment, and we'd wave back. People knew who we were. And the closer we got to Fort Lauderdale, the more surreal it all felt. The journey that once felt unreachable was now within our grasp. That's an emotional place to be—standing between a goal and its completion. Wanting it and not wanting it at the same time. So, stroke by stroke, we rowed on.

The weather was perfect. The Intracoastal was alive and shimmering. And for once, we weren't thinking about Miami or the end of the entire journey. Our only focus was reaching that marina—just one more step.

One more milestone. As we got closer to Fort Lauderdale, the shoreline changed. High-rises began stretching along the water—beautiful apartment buildings rising above the palm trees. It wasn't urban in the harsh sense, but it was definitely built up. More people. More energy. More activity. Different . . . but not bad. Just a new face of Florida.

The bridges became grander too—Spanish-style structures with little stucco bridge-tender houses perched over the water. We joked about stopping to fish under one of them. I still had this ridiculous daydream of catching a Florida fish before we finished, even though we were basically rowing through someone's waterfront neighborhood. But everything was just unbelievably beautiful.

For lunch, we didn't even stop rowing. We just rested the oars on our laps and drifted as we ate. It was like we were intentionally delaying arrival—wanting to get there but also feeling that bittersweet tug: When we reach the marina, we'll be incredibly close to the end. That push-pull emotion stayed with us all day. People still waved, hollered, cheered. The *Atlantic City* lettering on the side of the boat was our magnet.

Atlantic City experienced a new wave of excitement back home, a sort of rebirth, and people recognized the name instantly. Combine that with our story, and it made perfect sense why people gravitated toward us. The journey had a pulse now.

As we got closer, I said, "Kel, where is this marina?" We honestly couldn't tell how far we had left. We finally spotted a dock where people stood around.

We rowed over and asked, "Do you know how far the Bahia Mar Marina is?"

Their faces lit up. "Hey—you're those kids! The rowers!"

"Yep, that's us. How far is the marina?"

"You're only about three miles away. Straight ahead. Can't miss it."

That was the fuel we needed. We looked at each other. "This is it," I said.

"Yep," Kelly answered. "And don't forget—we gotta call home when we get there. Things could be happening." That reminder hung in the air.

Then we saw it—the Bahia Mar Marina. Over the top. Massive. Beautiful. Giant yachts lined up shoulder-to-shoulder; gleaming in all shapes and sizes. The heart of Fort Lauderdale boating life. Everything you'd picture when you think of a high-end Florida marina—it was that and more. We rowed into it like a thimble bobbing in a sea of mega-yachts.

Kelly said, "We've gotta check in with the harbormaster."

We tied up, climbed out, stretched our legs, and just stared. Total awe. How did two kids from Atlantic City end up here, of all places? We found the harbormaster, and he gave us the smile we'd seen a hundred times on the trip—the half-amused, half-impressed smile adults give when they don't quite know what to do with you.

"So . . . what do you boys want to do? Staying here?"

"We were hoping we could leave our boat here tonight," we said.

He raised his eyebrows. "You know how much people pay for slips here, right?"

"Yeah . . . we think we do."

He grinned. "Alright. Pull her over there. But I can't let you stay longer than two days, okay?" He was as nice as could be. We'd made it. We were in. Another milestone of the journey—checked off.

Having fun at our professional photo shoot
Photos taken by *The Miami News*

Tomorrow we head for the finish line
Photos taken by *The Miami News*

Chapter 16 -
More Than Miles

Kelly and I stood there in the middle of the Bahia Mar Marina, looking around like two kids who had wandered into the wrong movie set. We were cracking up, laughing, shaking our heads at the whole scene—giant yachts towering over us, polished chrome, teak decks, boat names written in gold leaf. And then, without us knowing, the harbormaster called the media. Of course we had no idea. We weren't thinking about publicity. We weren't thinking about attention. We were just overwhelmed by where we were. But apparently, the harbormaster thought we were newsworthy enough to call the *Sun Sentinel*.

So I turned to Kelly and said, "Okay, we gotta get ourselves together. And . . . it's time to make the call." He didn't want to. I knew he didn't want to. But our instructions were clear—call home when we reached Fort Lauderdale. So I laid it on thick. "Sorry, man. This is the plan. You gotta do it."

Kelly made the call. A few minutes later, he came back with a new number. "Our parents are already here," he said, stunned. "They're at a hotel nearby. They left this number."

He didn't know how they pulled it off—I certainly didn't. For all we knew, they'd been in Florida a day before we arrived. But they were already checked into a waterfront hotel, waiting. We went together to the marina phone—one of those classic payphones surrounded by guys working on their boats. Kelly dialed the number, and I think his mom picked up.

The moment she heard his voice, there was excitement in the background, voices talking over one another: "Where are you? We're down here! Where exactly are you?"

"We're at the Bahia Mar Marina," Kelly said.

We could hear the information getting relayed to his father. "I know where that is! Stay put. Don't go anywhere. We'll be there in forty minutes." They were in North Miami. And the coolest part? They deliberately booked a hotel on the water with docks, just in case we were able to row right up to it the next day. My father had been right—they had taken care of everything.

So now we waited. We were nervous, excited, anxious. We hadn't seen our parents in nearly three months. The only exception was when Mr. O'Neill flew his plane down earlier in the trip, landed somewhere near us, and surprised Kelly for a brief visit. But other than that—we'd been on our own.

While we were waiting, a man walked up to us. "You the kids rowing to Florida?"

"Yep."

He handed us a card. "I'm with the *Sun Sentinel*. Here's what I'd like to do . . ." He explained they wanted a photo shoot and a feature article. A full spread. We barely understood what that meant at the time. He also said he'd alert a local TV station—they might grab footage too. "Be here at ten tomorrow morning," he said. "Can't promise the TV crew, but the photographer will definitely be here." He was courteous, professional, straight to the point. Then he walked off, leaving us staring at each other like . . . What just happened?

But before long, we forgot all about the media. Because suddenly—there they were. Our families. They descended on the marina like a joyful mob—laughing, shouting our names, hugging us, touching our shoulders, gripping our arms like they couldn't believe we were real. They were overwhelmed. Shocked. Amazed to see us standing in the middle of this massive marina like two stray sailors who'd washed ashore. And then came the announcement: "We even got you boys your own room." It was the sweetest thing we'd heard in months.

We dragged our duffel bag—damp, moldy, smelling like three months of adventure—toward the rental car. The moms were horrified. The dads were amused. We crammed everyone in somehow and headed toward the hotel in North Miami where they were staying, which turned out to be really nice—waterfront, with docks, lounge chairs, a little beach area, and a cabana bar.

My father said, "We're taking you out to dinner tonight. Be ready at seven. And . . . you're not wearing that, are you?" Kelly and I looked at each other. What did we have to wear?

I said, "I have a yellow shirt with blue stripes." Kelly burst out laughing. My father didn't get the joke, but Kelly did—that shirt had become part of the mythology of the trip.

We emptied the duffel bag onto the bed. The mothers were horrified all over again. One of them bribed the hotel laundry staff to wash everything. We put on the cleanest, least-wrinkled clothes we could find. Kelly avoided the red sweatpants that night, thank God.

When we walked into the restaurant, something funny happened: the maître d' recognized us. "Oh! These are the boys? The rowers?"

My father proudly announced, "These are the kids that rowed down the coast." And just like that, the red carpet rolled out. The service, the smiles, the attention—it was like eating inside the final chapter of a feel-good movie. The dinner was incredible—not just because of the food but because we were surrounded by people who loved us. It was one of the best meals of the entire trip. So there we were—Kelly and I—standing in this hotel room with the shades pulled open, staring out at miles of open water, realizing we had absolutely no clue how we were supposed to end this whole adventure. Our parents were already here. People were expecting . . . something. Some kind of grand finish. Some kind of plan. And the truth was we didn't have one. All we knew was this: Tomorrow, we'd row again. And we'd figure out the ending when we got there. Kelly, of course, was calm as ever.

"It'll work out somehow," he said. I'm looking at him like, Yeah, I guess it will, but inside I'm thinking, We really should figure this out.

After waking up in the hotel the next morning during breakfast, we told our folks, "Hey, we've gotta be back at the marina before ten. We still have to get the boat ready—we're rowing today."

They nodded like that made perfect sense. Meanwhile, I'm thinking: We're rowing to the hotel . . . without half our stuff. This'll be interesting. When we got back to the marina, we thanked the harbormaster. (I still can't remember what they officially called him.) He'd lined everything up for us: the *Sun Sentinel*, the big paper.

Their guy shows up—top photographer, total pro, three cameras hanging off him like ornaments on a Christmas tree. He says, "This shoot should take an hour and a half." An hour and a half!? We were planning on rowing a full day! But we didn't say anything. We just smiled.

First came the interview. Kelly and I had a private laugh beforehand. I looked at him and said, "What's it gonna be this time—the whales?" He couldn't stop laughing. We decided to keep things straight this time. No embellishing. No sea monsters. Just the truth—who we were, what we were doing, and why. Then came the photo shoot. This guy was all over the marina—on the dock, on the stern of some giant boat, leaning at angles that defied gravity. He's telling us to row, then stop, then row again.

"Okay, now look back over your shoulder like this . . . climb into the boat this way . . ." It felt like we were in some nautical fashion show. Our parents were watching with their jaws on the ground.

"These are the kids we let loose from New Jersey?" You could almost hear them thinking it.

Then the news crew arrived. Now it was a full production—lights, cameras, microphones. Totally surreal. It was probably the most professional thing either of us had ever been part of. And honestly? It exhausted me more than rowing 40 miles. We finished up, exchanged cards, thanked everyone, and suddenly it was time to actually . . . row. But before we could escape, my Italian mother handed us enough food for three weeks. "Mom, we'll be gone five hours . . ." Didn't matter. Food was love.

We pushed off into the water feeling strangely light—because, for once, the duffel bag wasn't in the boat.

Neither was the tent, nor the stove. All of it was already at the hotel. It felt like rowing in a dream—smooth, easy, almost effortless. The harbormaster came out and gave us a thumbs up. We waved back like this was something we did every weekend. As we rowed out, Kelly and I started laughing again.

"You know," I said, "we still don't know where we're ending this thing."

"Yeah," he said, "we don't."

"The hotel is actually located in the Miami area, and we're rowing there today. Nobody knows that."

"Nope. Not a soul." We figured we'd just pick a good spot to finish and make it official. Our parents only had a day or two left, so honestly—why drag this out? We'd reached Miami. Our goal was already met. Now it was just a matter of creating the moment.

The day's row was beautiful—classic Intracoastal scenery, all that South Florida sparkle. We reached the hotel dock, and there were our families, sitting at the outdoor bar, cheering like we'd just won the Olympics. We tied up, got cleaned up, and finally sat down to figure out the endgame. We called the media guy and told him we'd pick a spot for tomorrow—something close, maybe a park six miles away. There were plenty of bayside parks where cars could pull in, and they'd look great on camera. We just needed a place that was undeniably Miami. Tomorrow would be it. Our dream finale. The journey that began in Atlantic City would finally get its ending—one we'd somehow craft out of sun, sweat, adrenaline, and whatever magic had followed us these entire two and a half months.

Once we were back to the hotel, and what struck me immediately was how much fun our parents were having.

It was like, after two and a half months of worrying about us, praying for us, imagining the worst—they finally got to step into our world for a moment. They laughed, hung out by the water, relaxing. And honestly, that might have been my favorite part of the whole ending, or the beginning of the ending. Seeing them get a taste of the dream we'd been living. We unloaded whatever gear we had left, and that somehow nearly took over the hotel.

They let us stash things in the employees' area—our lamp, our lantern, the camping stove—like it was our own personal storage closet. Just another example of the way strangers along the journey kept giving us generosity we never deserved. While we unloaded, my father kept waving the business cards at me like a conductor keeping the orchestra on tempo.

"Don't forget to call the media guy. Don't forget."

"All right, Dad, I won't. Relax." I finally called the guy and told him the plan: "This is it. The end. We picked a public park about six miles across the bay. That's where we'll make our triumphant arrival." I didn't say "MacArthur-esque," though the thought crossed my mind. He thanked me for the info but didn't exactly confirm whether anyone was showing up. One more thing checked off the list.

Back in the room, we showered—no need to shave, we'd given up on that weeks ago—and cleaned ourselves up for our final night with our parents. We went out to dinner again, and once more, our parents pointed at us like they were unveiling a gift. "These are the guys who rowed thirteen hundred miles." And again, the same reaction: friendly people, big smiles, lots of disbelief. We got tucked in a corner where we could talk and soak in the moment. It was just good to sit with the people who'd supported us through the whole thing, the ones who made this even possible.

Everyone kept reminding us: "Tomorrow's the day."

"Tomorrow's the finish."

And we nodded along, pretending to be relaxed, but inside we were buzzing. That night, lying on the bed and staring at the ceiling, my mind was too crowded to sleep. It wasn't nerves, exactly—it was more like realizing that two and a half months of adventure were about to collapse into one final moment.

Morning came. We had a solid breakfast and gave our parents the plan, the timing, the location. The boat was lighter than ever—almost too light. It hadn't been this empty since the day we first tested it out on the water. But one thing stood in our way: a twenty-mile-an-hour headwind blasting across open water.

"Well . . . I guess this is fitting," I told Kelly. Part of the deal. Part of the story. We pushed off anyway.

The first few strokes felt bizarre—the boat was so empty that it practically skipped across the waves. It was like trying to balance a cork in a bathtub. The wind blew hard enough to slap the oars around. The whole thing was messy, uncomfortable, and not at all the serene glide I'd imagined. In my fantasy version of that day, the water was supposed to be perfectly calm. Pelicans would guide us like heavenly ushers. Dolphins would escort us in formation. Maybe even an angelic spotlight breaking through the clouds. But what we got instead was chaos. Bouncing, rocking, fighting the wind, trying to keep the boat facing the right direction. More humbling than triumphant. Yet we pressed on.

The island was visible now, close enough to make out the shoreline. But as we approached, something became clear: there were no crowds. No banners. No reporters (at least none visible). No tourists even wandering around. Just our parents. Waving. Calling out, "We're here!" And that was it. For a moment, disappointment tried to creep in. This is how we're ending it? After everything? But the closer we got, the more another thought settled in my mind: This is exactly how it started. No fanfare. No cameras. No fireworks or cannons. Just two kids pushing off with a handful of friends watching. And now, two and a half months later, we were pulling into Miami the same way we left Atlantic City. Full circle. After all those miles, all those people cheering us on along the East Coast, all the strangers who had heard the story . . . This was the grand finale. Four parents and one cameraman leaning against a seawall. That was it.

As we got closer, we heard clapping and cheering, but it was only coming from our folks. The water was rough, the wind still ripped through the channel, and even getting out of the boat was a challenge. We tied it up while it banged around, both of us wobbling, trying not to fall in during what was supposed to be our triumphant finish. It wasn't glamorous. It was awkward, windy, and messy. But as soon as we stepped onto that seawall, it felt like exactly the way it was meant to be—because it was how we'd started.

We spent the next hour celebrating. Our parents had grabbed champagne on the way, and we ended up spraying it around more than drinking it. We laughed, we soaked it in, and slowly accepted that this—this tiny little moment with just the six of us—was the ending God had written. And honestly? It was enough. More than enough. Our parents had flown all the way down to support us. That alone was a gift. We wouldn't have had anyone cheering if they hadn't shown up. Kelly and I both felt it: deep thankfulness. Gratitude that the people who mattered most were here. There were tears from our mothers, hugs, and all the emotions finally catching up.

Then the guy from the TV Station came over and said, "I didn't really get a good shot of you coming in. The glare was bad. Think you could row back out and come in again?" Only on our trip could something like that happen.

We looked at each other, laughed, and said, "Yeah. Sure. Why not?"

By then the wind had eased up a little. So we rowed out and decided to give him the entrance. Total synchronization. Perfect stroke rhythm. The sun hit us just right. We slid into the shoreline like champions. He gave us a thumbs up, tossed his equipment in the car, and drove off. Just like that—our "crowd" was down by one again.

Then my dad—who had been waiting his turn—said, "I want to take a row."

We couldn't help it. We burst out laughing. "Don't get lost!"

"Don't go too far!"

"Point the boat the right way, Dad!"

He went out, fought the wind for a minute, and came straight back. But the whole thing was pure joy. We were just being ourselves—no performance, no pretending. Just family. My mom brought food, of course, and we ate while they told us how proud they were. Honestly, they were seeing the reactions we'd gotten for weeks—but they were seeing it fresh. We were used to it by then. It had become normal to us. But to them, it was like watching a movie they didn't know their kids starred in.

Eventually they had to leave. Flights at seven, preparations to make. We said our goodbyes. More tears. More hugs. My mom pulled me aside, slipped money into my hand, and said, "You might need this. And hopefully you'll be home for Christmas."

That got me. My dad grabbed my hand next—another handshake, another folded bill tucked into my palm. "This might come in handy," he said. They hadn't coordinated it. It was just who they were. Their own way of blessing us.

I looked back at my mom and dad, and my mind began to drift. It carried me to another time—when I was small, and they held me steady in the sand and guided me through the water. Those moments had quietly shaped me, forming a foundation I hadn't fully understood until now. Standing there, it felt as though something had come full circle, as if life had its own quiet way of returning what was first given. And in that realization, there was a gentle sense that things were unfolding just as they were meant to. And then they were gone.

Kelly and I stood there alone on the shore, looking at each other. We hugged. We did our traditional claw-hand shake. And then we realized . . . we actually had to row back to the hotel. But by then the wind had calmed. The water smoothed out. And as soon as we looked out . . . there they were. Dolphins. I nudged Kelly.

"This is our cue."

They didn't follow us all the way back, but it was like they saluted us as we rowed past them. The row took an hour, maybe two. The sun dropped lower. The day was settling, soft and quiet. And as we rowed, we started reminiscing—almost instinctively. Every face, every act of kindness, every moment that sustained us:

The man in Sea Isle who gave us his apartment.

Our friends' parents who gave us their house in Cape May.

A Catholic priest who saved us and helped us in our time of need.

The woman who brought groceries because we reminded her of her son.

The countless people who fed us, housed us, guided us, protected us.

One memory after another. A flood of gratitude. I felt my eyes start to sting. Blamed the sun at first. But it wasn't the sun.

Kelly looked at me and said quietly, "We had to have had an angel watching over us. After everything we went through . . . there had to be an angel."

I didn't answer because I couldn't. And because he was right—just not in the way he meant it. It wasn't one angel. It was an army of angels. Every person we met along the way had been part of that army. Each one sent at the right moment, for the right need, with the right blessing. We just kept rowing after that, without many more words. Letting the reality settle in. And that's how the dream ended. Quietly. Beautifully. Full of gratitude, full of God's fingerprints, full of faces we'll never forget.

I'll leave everyone with the verse that sums it all up: "Do not forget to entertain strangers, for by doing so some have entertained angels without knowing it" (Hebrews 13:2).

The perfect ribbon on the journey God wrote for us.

Rowing into the North Miami hotel

Taking time to goof around at our hotel

Preparations for our final strokes to the finish

We made it!

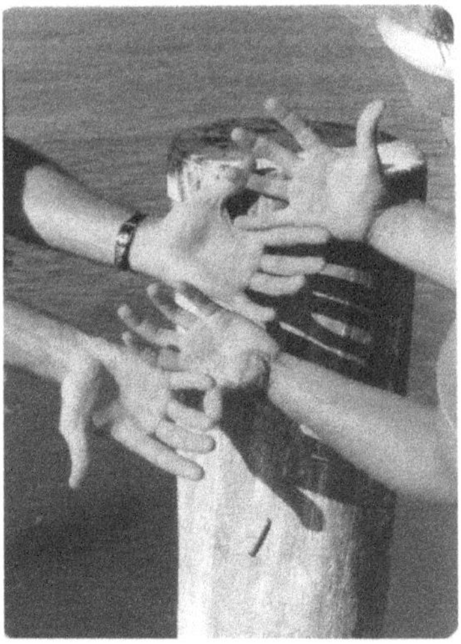

True Blister Brothers

POINTS OF INTEREST

1. After officially landing: Rowed to a campsite in the Upper Keys
2. Kelly traveled home to Atlantic City to pick up his truck/camper with boat trailer and back to Florida in less than eight days.
3. Arrived home two days before Christmas, which made my mother very happy.
4. Having stayed in camp for over a week awaiting Kelly's return, had continued bad luck with my Florida fishing experience; although, I did hook a nice fish that spooled most of my line.
5. Atlantic City presented us with Letters of Accommodation and Medals for positive attention given to the city throughout our journey—by the way, no whales were mentioned in the presentation.
6. Kelly put together a program from our limited movie film presenting our rowing trip for our local students as well as many business groups.
7. I graduated Stockton College in 1980 and married Terry in 1987.
8. Kelly moved to Florida and still lives there today with his wife, Laurie.
9. It's interesting that Kelly has raised his family and has lived onboard a sailboat for over forty years.
10. On all of our Florida vacations, which have been numerous, I still haven't landed a tarpon.

"A ship in harbor is safe,
but that's not what ships are built for."
John A Shedd

Medal presented to us by Edwin J. Roth—
Atlantic City Commissioner at the time
(ACBP Award)

After our adventure, the third member of our crew, *Old #10*, had to go back to work.

THE 1978 MUSICAL GROUPS FOR AN EXCELLENT PLAYLIST

1. Steely Dan
2. The Who
3. Crosby, Stills, & Nash
4. Neil Young
5. Grin
6. Eagles
7. David Bowie
8. Mott the Hoople
9. Rolling Stones
10. Dire Straits
11. Beatles
12. 10CC
13. Roxy Music
14. Electric Light Orchestra
15. Grand Funk Railroad
16. Humble Pie
17. Little Feat
18. James Gang
19. Mountain
20. Wishbone Ash

NOTE:
If you are going to row a boat 1,300 miles, this *must* be included—

Richard Wagner
"Ride of the Valkyries"

www.ingramcontent.com/pod-product-compliance
Lightning Source LLC
LaVergne TN
LVHW012138100626
840942LV00009B/14
9781967386581